Book 1
Circuit Engineering
By Solis Tech

&

Book 2
Malware
By Solis Tech

Book 1
Circuit Engineering

By Solis Tech

The Beginner's Guide to Electronic Circuits, Semi-Conductors, Circuit Boards, and Basic Electronics

Table of Contents

Introduction..5

Chapter I – First Things First: An Introduction to Circuit Engineering.................6

Chapter II – The Anatomy of a Circuit,,,...12

Chapter III – Resistance Isn't Futile...16

Chapter IV – It's Time to Measure the Electric Flow in a Circuit.........................21

Chapter V – Power Transfer at Max...23

Chapter VI – Laws, Laws & More Laws..30

Chapter VII – Understanding Electromagnetism..36

Chapter VIII – Let's Talk Circuit Boards..40

Chapter IX – Sufficient Safety...44

Chapter X – Here's a Multimeter for You!..47

Chapter XI - DIY Circuits: Simple Projects..50

Chapter XII – Making Your Way to Circuit Design: PCB Layouts & Schematic Diagrams...61

Chapter XIII – A Way Is through EDA...71

Chapter XIV – The Other Way around: Reverse Engineering...............................74

Chapter XV – Hacking the System...78

Chapter XVI – Advanced Circuit Engineering: Microcontrollers & Robots.........83

Conclusion..87

Introduction

I want to thank you and congratulate you for purchasing the book, **Circuit Engineering: The Beginner's Guide to Electronic Circuits, Semi-Conductors, Circuit Boards, and Basic Electronics**.

This book contains a beginner's course on circuit engineering. Here, the basics of electric and electronic circuits are discussed. You will grasp the definitions of circuits, semi-conductors, resistors, inductors, transformers, circuit boards, and electronics, in general. You'll even be introduced to electrical safety tips and a set of skills needed in electronics, as well as a short take on reverse engineering, hacking, microcontroller programming, and robotics.

Alongside, you can apply all that you'll be learning once you get started with the proposed circuit projects for beginner. You'll also be rewarded a peek at different career-advancement possibilities. While reading about the fundamentals and various theories in the subject is important, hands-on learning is equally important. This way, you can put your newly gathered knowledge to good use.

If you're uncertain whether or not you have what it takes to learn the ropes in circuit engineering, let this book help you decide. Chances are, you have the stamina for the field and for all you know, you can discover a new passion for circuits and electronic devices.

Thanks again for purchasing this book; I hope you enjoy it!

Chapter I – First Things First: An Introduction to Circuit Engineering

In 1882, there was a *circuit war*; it was between the notable electrical engineers and scientists, *Thomas Edison* (inventor of the DC system) and *Nikola Tesla* (inventor of the AC system).

While Thomas Edison stated that an efficient way of distributing power was via a *DC system*, Nikola Tesla argued that although DC systems are efficient, an *alternating current* is the *more practical* option. It started as a simple clash of ideas, but it eventually led to a major rift. Neither professional conceded; both of them insisted that their own systems were "better".

In the end, it was *Nikola Tesla* that took home the *glory*. Case in point? He was granted funds by an internationally recognized firm, Westinghouse. The majority of the power sources of New York City were based on the ideas of the Serbian engineer; at Niagara Falls in Canada, a power plant was built.

If you're interested in finding out more about the particular *circuit war, AC and DC systems,* and all critical discussions on circuits, taking a course about electronic circuits is the way to go.

I.A. - What Is a Circuit?

Both an *electric circuit* and an *electronic circuit* refer to a complete pathway for electric current, which starts and ends at a single point; it is a passage that allows the electricity to enter at one place, then, let it pass through a series of stops, and finally, leave it to exit at the same place. The list of basic examples of a circuit includes a *light switch* (off and on) and *battery-operated lamps*.

A circuit that follows a fundamental design

A circuit can function well - granted that its design is well-conceptualized. As much as possible, it is recommended that arriving at a simplistic product should be the goal; the simple and straightforward a design is, the better. With a fundamental concept, even if other (beginner-level) circuit engineers who will subject it to inspection will not have a difficult time in understanding its flow. Although there may be complex systems, the agenda is not intended to complicate the explanations.

Moreover, a circuit can be referred to as a space with a conductive path that grants electrons the opportunity to move freely. To create one with a brilliant design, a tip is to learn about the classifications of all circuits. You can use the knowledge to determine the appropriate kind of network, as well as the need for an external or internal source.

2 classifications of a circuit:

1. Linear or non-linear – a circuit that is based on either linear or non-linear networks; it is composed of independent and/or dependent sources and passive elements

2. Active or passive – a circuit that is based on either the absence (passive circuit) or the presence (active circuit) of a source; a source can be a power source or voltage source

I.B. - A Circuit & Its Types

Not all circuits are alike. In fact, one of the most common misconceptions involves an *electric circuit* and an *electronic circuit*; both are said to be one and the same, but they are not. While the former can carry *average to high voltage*, the latter has the tendency to have *low voltage load*.

Moreover, it is always important to be aware of the different circuit types, especially if you're about to make your own circuit; the kind of circuit that you create needs to have the ability to handle a preferred load.

Circuit types:

- Closed circuit – it is a circuit that is fully functional

- Open circuit – it is a circuit that can no longer function due to a damaged or missing component, or a loose connection

- Short circuit – it is a circuit that comes without a load

- Parallel circuit – it is a circuit that connects to other circuits; it is like the main power source or the primary circuit in a series of circuits

- Series circuit – it is a circuit that connects to other circuits; the same amount of electricity is distributed to each of its component circuits; the main power source or the primary circuit is unclear

I.C. - Conductors, Insulators & Semi-Conductors

Conductors, insulators, and *semi-conductors* give light to the fact that a circuit's electrical properties are dependent on the circuit type, as well as on their conduction bands (i.e. their allowed electric power). For instance, if a particular power source chooses to distribute a 9-volt electric power to a closed circuit, its electrical properties can be evaluated by using 2 details: (1) its characteristic as a closed circuit and (2) 9-volt electric power.

Moreover, conductors, insulators, and semi-conductors are integral concepts to the *conductivity* of an object. While conductors and semi-conductors are grouped to describe *charged carriers*, insulators are still considered as relative despite not containing any free charge.

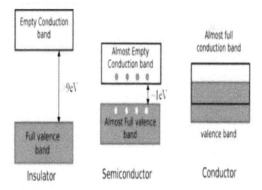

Insulators can be any "ion-less" object; the most common examples of semi-conductors are copper and aluminum & for conductors, gold and silver

Conduction bands:

- Conductor – it is a conduction band that is referred to as the almost full band

- Insulator – it is a conduction band that is referred to as an empty band

- Semi-conductor –it is a conduction band that is referred to as an almost empty band

I.D. - Breaking Down the Components of a Circuit

A circuit can be either *simple or complex*, and be both *simple and complex*. If the circuit in subject is a series circuit, with a group of 10 different circuits that are connected to it or if the said circuit is just a basic closed circuit with 5 different stops, it can be rather confusing to trace. However, if you dissect any circuit, you'll discover 3 *constant*, integral components.

Integral components:

1. Load – it is the representation of the power consumption, as well as the work that is accomplished within a system; without it, there's barely a point in having a circuit

2. Power source – it is where the electricity comes from

3. Pathway – it is the framework of a circuit; from the power source, it follows the load through each of the network, and finally returns to

and exits the power source; it is also referred to as the conductive pathway

I.E. - The Roles of Current, Resistance & Voltage

Current, resistance, and voltage are the 3 representations of the important components of a circuit's system. They can explain how electricity enters, then, moves from 1 point to another, and finally exits. Whether the path of electricity is rather simple, these representations remain constant. Apart from describing the electric flow, they can serve as indications of faults (in instances when a circuit fails to work).

3 representations:

- Current – it is the representation of the electric flow; particularly, its focus is on the flow of electrons

- Resistance – it is the representation of the nature of an electric flow as it moves around the circuit

- Voltage – it is the representation of the electric force or pressure; in general, the supply comes from an electric outlet or a battery

I.F. - AC/DC Systems: Which System Is in?

AC and DC systems (or alternating current and direct current systems) are often associated to each other. When the *AC system* is mentioned, so is the *DC system*. Conversely, when it's the DC system's turn to be in the spotlight, it won't be long until the AC system is mentioned. This is because these systems are opposite of one another; to get a better understanding of one of them, it's recommended to be familiar with the other, as well.

Moreover, *AC and DC systems* are types of a circuit's current flow. In an AC system, the current flow changes its direction occasionally. Meanwhile, in a DC system, the current flow follows a single direction.

It can be deduced, therefore, that an AC system grants a circuit freedom to let the current flow in several directions. While this can be an advantage, this doesn't permit the continuous flow that a DC system can entitle.

So, should you use an *AC system* or a *DC system*? The decision as to which current system is dependent on the more practical design to follow; take into account the aim of having your own circuit. If you prefer something grand and you intend to power something large, the AC system can step in. On the other hand, if you're good with a basic setup, you can use the DC system's concept as basis.

I.G. – What Is a Transformer?

A *transformer* is a device that serves as a portal for energy transfer within the points in a circuit or from circuit 1 to circuit 2. In most cases, it is used for increasing and decreasing the voltages in a system.

When the first transformer was built in the mid 1880s, circuit engineers discovered that a transformer significantly improves the electric flow in a circuit, and consequently, results to a more powerful circuit. The discovery made way for various transformer designs, as well as various transformer sizes.

A primary principle of a transformer is its need for extremely *high magnetic permeability*. It follows that a circuit that is capable of attracting power is, of course, more inclined to have electric current transferred to it; and, conversely, a circuit with *low magnetic permeability* is less likely to extract power from another circuit.

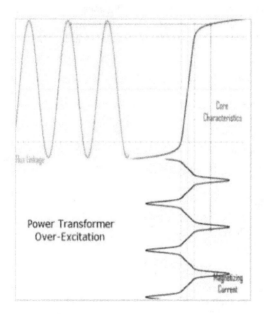

Magnetic permeability is defined as the ability of a circuit to hold and support an internal magnetic field

Chapter II – The Anatomy of a Circuit

Let's say that a lamp in your room has been around for a while, and let's say it chose to give up on you the other night; although it's an old lamp, you still believe it can *work fine.* You suspect that the problem is in the switching board. Instead of just letting it be and since you're interested in how it works, you choose to study its components.

As you open its internal system, you see that connected to some sort of panel are 2 wires; one wire is red, the other is black. As far as your knowledge in circuits can tell you, the 2 wires in your hands are: (1) a live wire or the wire that is connected to a switch, and (2) a neutral wire or the wire that carries the load.

As the universal rule in circuit engineering goes, *red* is the color that indicates a live wire, *black*, on the other hand, is a neutral wire. For a chance to know why your lamp gave up on you other than old age, checking the red wire would be a good start.

II.A. – Individually Speaking: Parts of a Circuit

A circuit can *work smoothly* if its individual parts are contributing to the workflow as expected. Remember that it follows a series; if one point in that series is not in condition. So, if you're wondering why a system is functional, check each one of its components. To use the old adage (and modify it a bit), the circuit, as a whole, is just as good as its individual parts.

Individual parts:

- Capacitor – it is in charge of the stability in the power source in a circuit

- Diode – it is in charge of supplying the light in a circuit

- Inductor – it is a coil of wiring system

- Resistor – it is in charge of power consumption

- Transistor – it is in charge of the electric signal control

II.B. – Circuit Categories: Which Category Do You Belong to?

Circuit categories describe the *voltage levels*, as well as their *electric flow over time*; they refer to how much and how powerful the current is as it enters and passes through each point in a circuit. Since they vary, it's listed as an effective way of understanding circuit systems of sorts if they are categorized.

Circuit categories:

- Analog circuits – these are the categories of circuits that use the concepts of parallel circuits and series circuits as basis. Among their fundamental parts are capacitors, diodes, resistors, and wires.

  In diagrams, analog circuits are easy to recognize. Usually, when a model of the particular circuit is drawn, a simple illustration is presented since these circuits do not follow a complex system. In most cases, when illustrated, the parts (e.g. capacitors, diodes, wires, etc.) are represented by lines.

- Digital circuits – these are the circuits that rely heavily on Boolean algebra (i.e. values are either true or false, or as denoted 1 or 0); therefore, these circuits are often dependent on transistors that can create closed logic. Compared to analog circuits, these follow a state-of-the-art design.

  Furthermore, digital circuits are designed to create either numerical or logical values for the representation of electricity that flows within their system. Since these are not only focused on the mere ability to take in electric current, but rather, on the individual properties of all of their parts, as well, these circuits come with advanced functions; they can provide memory and accomplish arbitrary computations.

- Analog-digital – these circuits are sometimes called hybrid circuits or mixed signal circuits since both system designs of analog and digital circuits are given light. Although their concept can be quite complex, these circuits can deliver a more thorough result; the procedures are combined, which allows collaborative effort from different parts. One example is a telephone receiver; first, it works based on analog circuitry to create and stabilize signals, then, based on digital circuitry, these signals are converted into digital units, and finally, are subjected to interpretation.

II.C. – Where Does Inductance Enter the Picture?

In circuit analysis, the term *inductance*, introduced in 1886 by *Oliver Heaviside*, refers to the property of a circuit's electricity-producing component to change in amount. Apart from the support of a circuit's aspect to vary, it points out the need for a filter and energy storage systems to be provided.

As it follows, the component in a circuit that enables inductance is called an inductor. Usually, these parts are made out of wire. But, while some circuits contain inductors as integral parts, others remain functional without the need to alter the electric flow.

Inductance can be either *mutual inductance* or *self-inductance*. The former refers to a change in electric current from one inductor to another inductor; it explains the primary operations of a transformer. Meanwhile, the latter refers to the *stable inductance* within a system.

Moreover, inductance is represented by the symbol *L*, which is meant to giver to the scientist, *Heinrich Lenz*. It also measured in units of *henry* after the American scientist, *Joseph Henry*; it follows that although it was Oliver Heaviside who introduced the term, the man behind the development is Joseph Henry.

Mutual inductance describes the occurrence in a circuit when there is change that can be traced to an inductor; particularly, it refers to the alteration due to an inductor's preference of a nearby inductor. It is essential to learn about the relationship of *2 inductors* since it is the basis of the operations of a transformer. Additionally, a limit has to be maintained in order to keep potential energy transfers regulated; the failure to incorrectly calculate mutual inductance can result to *unwanted inductance coupling*, as well as a *power overload*.

It can, therefore, be deduced that mutual inductance (as represented by the symbol *M*) is the measurement of the coupling that involves 2 inductors; the 2 inductors are, then, given particular importance (in terms of coil turns), along with each inductor's ability to admit current flow or *permeance*. The formula for calculating mutual inductance is as follows:

**representations: M_{AB} = mutual inductance in circuit A and circuit B

N_B = inductance in circuit B

N_A = inductance in circuit A

P_{AB} = permeability in circuit A and circuit B

$$M_{AB} = (N_B)(N_A)(P_{AB})$$

When explained, the formula highlights that the mutual inductance between inductor A and inductor B (or M_{AB}) is equal to the product of 3 elements: [1] the coils of inductor B (or N_B), [2] the coils of inductor A (or N_A), and [3] the permeance of inductor A and inductor B (or P_{AB}).

On the other hand, self-inductance refers to voltage induction of a current-carrying system in respect to the changing current in the circuit. It points out that eventually, there will be another current that will flow along with the primary current. Due to the amount of force within the magnetic field, voltage is induced; particularly, voltage is *self-induced.*

II.D. - What Makes an Integrated Circuit?

An *integrated circuit* (or IC) is alternatively called a microchip or a chip, due to its size. It works depending on a particular signal level. One example is the integrated circuit that enables a computer to perform a multitude of tasks; instead of loading a computer's structure with a large circuit, it comes to the rescue.

In most cases, an *integrated circuit* operates at little defined states. Compared to the normal circuit whose operations are distributed over continuous amplitudes, it can function within a small network; the normal circuit may sometimes fail to work with only minor amplitude ranges.

Basically, an *integrated circuit* is no different from any other circuit; its power can astound you, yes, but, if it comes down to describing how it is, it's simply a circuit that has been reduced so it can fit inside a chip.

Chapter III – Resistance Isn't Futile

Without a material that can act as the opposing force, a circuit can *function*, but it may not function *as desired*. When an electric supply can perform its function by distributing electricity to the opening of a circuit, the electric current will keep on flowing; its flow can be uncontrollable, which can destroy a system's integrity. Usually, without the opposition, a circuit ends up taking too much load.

The term for this opposing material is *resistance*; it goes hand in hand with the term conductance. And, as mentioned in the first chapter, it is the representation of the current flow in a circuit.

III.A. – What Is Resistance?

Resistance is the measurement of an opposing electric current; it can be expressed in ohms. It generates an amount of friction that is relative to the necessary amount of electricity that a particular circuit can handle.

In a way, *resistance* is responsible for the *smooth flow of electricity* in a circuit. Although others would counter the argument by saying that rather than support the effortless flow of electricity in a system, it slows it down.

However, it is *resistance* that allows *balance of electricity* in a circuit. Take for example the case of a circuit that can only handle a total of 15V. If a circuit takes in 20V at a resistance of 5 ohms, the number is diminished to 15V, which indicates a functional circuit. Conversely, if, in the same situation, there is no *resistance* of 5 ohms, a circuit may not be as functional as desired; its system ends up carrying 20V, which implies that it is overloaded.

III.B. – Resistive Circuit 101

A *resistive circuit* is a kind of circuit that consists of nothing but a series of resistors to complete the combo of electric current and voltage source. If viewed in a chart, it is noticeable that the power waveform is always positive; it is suggestive the power in a circuit is always dissipated, and is never returned to the original source.

It is important to note that the frequency of the power in a circuit should not be equal to the frequency of the electric current and voltage. If possible, the frequency of the power should be twice as high as that of the electric current and voltage. This unequal frequency distribution grants constant change within a system.

Since it is made up of resistors and does not include transistors and capacitors, a resistive circuit is rather easier to analyze. Understanding the electric flow within the circuit (whether in an AC or DC system) requires a straightforward technique. Therefore, determining the flow of the current in a resistive circuit is simple; by adhering to the formula, calculating the figure is easy.

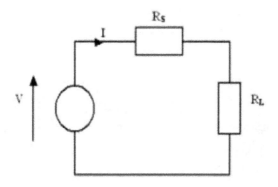

In a resistive circuit, voltage can easily be monitored

**representations: I = total current

RS = Resistance Source

RL = Resistance Load

I = voltage ÷ (RS +RL)

III.C. - War between the Types of Resistance

Resistance is classified according to the type of resistivity that it can contain, along with the amount of resistance that a circuit can carry. This allows the opportunity for an opposing force to be valued, regardless of its resistivity. As the professional electrical engineers can attest, not every circuit component that produces resistance satisfies the rules, particularly, *Ohm's Law.*

2 types of resistance:

- Differential resistance – it is the resistance derivative of voltage in light with the electric current; also referred to as *incremental resistance, small signal resistance, or dynamic resistance,* its concept is responsible for oscillators and amplifiers

- Static resistance – it is the resistance that corresponds to the typical definition of resistance; it is also called *chordal resistance* or *DC resistance*

III.D. - Resistance vs. Conductance

The average circuit comes with both *resistance* and *conductance*, which gives balance to the electric flow in a circuit's system. While the former refers to the opposition, conductance describes the amount of current that is converted into power that revolves around different points.

Conductance also covers the ability of a circuit's components to conduct electricity. And, to bring light to its counterpart's ability to oppose the flow, it dwells on the subject of the convenience of electricity to pass through a series of points in a circuit.

With both the resistance and the conductance in the system, a circuit can function as desired.

III.E. – The Need for Calculations (Four Ways)

For electric current to flow smoothly within a system, a level of resistance has to be present. And, since not all circuits come with a similar design, their resistance levels vary. To calculate a particular circuit's resistance, first, you need determine its type, and its provided values, as well.

Four ways:

#1 – Resistance calculation for a series circuit

The formula:

Resistance = $_1R + _2R + _3R + _4R$

#2 – Resistance calculation according to voltage & power

**representations: total voltage; PT = total power

The formula:

Resistance = $VT^2 \div PT^2$

3 – Resistance calculation according to voltage & current

**representations: VT = total voltage; IT = total current

The formula:

Resistance = VT ÷ IT

4 – Resistance calculation according to power & current

**representations: PT = total power; IT = total current

The formula:

Resistance = PT ÷ IT

III.F. – What about Sheet Resistance?

Sheet resistance refers to the measurement of the resistance in a thin sheet in a circuit's components. It can be used to describe the resistibility of different circuits and can point out the specific difference in circuits that vary in size. Especially in the case of a commercial product, the topic is covered for the assurance of quality.

You can look at *sheet resistance* as a special kind of resistance since it generates a more specific value. Usually, the average resistance in a circuit is expressed in *ohms*; *sheet resistance* is expressed in *Ohms per square*.

In most cases, *sheet resistance* is used for the analysis of circuits with uniform conductivity or semi-conductivity. Typical applications are extended to quality assurance for a commercial circuit.

III.G. – The Role of Impedance & Admittance

Like resistance, *impedance* can be described as the opposition in a circuit; unlike resistance, however, it refers to the opposing force of a circuit after the application of voltage. It is only relevant to AC systems or circuits where direct current isn't the supplied.

It was in 1893 when the concept of *impedance* was initially introduced by the Irish engineer, Arthur Kenelly. Back then, it was denoted by Z and is defined as a complex number.

When it comes to quantitative terms, *impedance* refers to the ratio of voltage to the electric current in a circuit. Its introduction is important for beginners especially if they're scratching their heads as to why there's an opposing force besides resistance.

Impedance, like resistance, comes with values. In a single open circuit, its value is presented in *ohms*. In the event of a series circuit or a parallel circuit, its value can be calculated by simply adding all the defined values in each unit.

The formula:

**representations: TZ = total impedance

Z_1 = impedance in component 1

Z_2 = impedance in component 2

Z_3 = impedance in component 3

Z_{10} = impedance in final component of a circuit

$$TZ = Z_1 + Z_2 + Z_3 \dots Z_n$$

Meanwhile, *admittance* is a relative concept in circuit engineering. It addresses the issue that alongside the difference in the magnitude of the electric current and voltage that are flowing within a circuit, the difference in phases needs to be given light, too. This way, the maximum load within a system can be calculated accordingly.

The formula:

**representations: TY = total admittance

Y_1 = admittance in component 1

Y_2 = admittance in component 2

Y_3 = admittance in component 3

Y_{10} = admittance in final component of a circuit

$$TY = Y_1 + Y_2 + Y_3 \dots Y_n$$

Chapter IV – It's Time to Measure the Electric Flow in a Circuit

In the previous chapter, the formulas for the calculation of a circuit's resistance levels were shared. However, the formulas for the *calculation of the entire load* in a circuit have yet to be discussed.

This is due to the significance of using the appropriate measurement units. In a few cases, especially those who are still on the initial phase of learning circuits? They aren't quite careful with their selected units. As it follows, it's not only necessary to calculate a circuit's electric flow; it's also necessary to calculate a circuit's flow correctly.

IV.A. – Standard Units

Among the several reasons to use *standard units of measurement* are for indications of exact measurements and for indications of the preferred measurements in a system. These units bring uniformity.

In circuits, the usual standard units that you encounter are *V, W, I,* and *P.* Although there are more, those who wish to explain a system's electric flow rely on these measurements; rather than introduce a bunch, which may only make matters more confusing, some are preferred. Moreover, without such units, understanding others' discussions of circuits is nearly impossible.

Standard units:

- Conductance – its measuring unit is Siemen with G as symbol

- Current – its measuring unit is ampere with I or i as symbol

- Frequency – its measuring unit is Hertz with Hz as symbol

- Inductance – its measuring unit is Henry with H or L as symbol

- Power – its measuring is watts with W as symbol

- Resistance – its measuring unit is ohm with R as symbol

- Voltage – its measuring unit is volt with V or E as symbol

IV.B. – Commonly Used Alternatives

Other than the *standard units of measurement,* other units are given light since these can enable clearer expression of the electric flow in a circuit. Especially if the circuit in subject contains a rather complex system, it can be difficult to arrive at a definite solution.

Other units:

- Angular frequency – it is a unit of measurement used in an AC circuit; it is a rotational unit that describes the relationship of at least 2 electric forms in a circuit

- Decibel – it is a unit of measurement that represent the gain in either current, power, or voltage; since it is only a tenth of the original unit, *Bel*, it is primarily reserved for denoting extremely small amounts

- Time constant – it is a unit of measurement that describes the output of a circuit's minimum or maximum output value; in a way, it refers to the measurement of time reaction

- Watt-hour – it is the unit of measurement that describes the electrical energy consumption over a period of time

IV.C. – Units of Force

Since *force* in a circuit is an important concept, it is advised that the particular unit of measurement is presented correctly. Even in physics, it is reiterated that it should be labeled according to its right category.

Atomic and electrostatic units of force:

- Hartrees

- Newtons

- Tesla

- Coulombs

- Meters

Chapter V – Power Transfer at Max

There will be instances of a *power transfer* in a circuit. For the electricity to continue its smooth flow, its original energy source will be replaced with an internal energy source. With such a change (especially in the case of a series circuit where power needs to flow continuously), the explanation for its system's pattern becomes a notch challenging.

For *beginners*, a great way of understanding *power transfer* in a circuit is to understand maximum power transfer, along with the concepts that dwell on the topic. As it follows, by gaining clarity on how much was the original power, as well as how much power a particular circuit can handle, you can see whether a power transfer is necessary or will only cause its load to be compromised.

V.A. – Maximum Power Transfer

Maximum power transfer, a concept that was introduced by Moritz von Jacobi sometime in the 1840s, draws light on the idea that for maximum external power to be obtained, an internal resistance needs to be in place. However, the transfer can only be flawless if the original resistance is equal to the potential power that an internal resistor can produce.

Consequently, maximum power transfer yields results that point out *power transfer*, and not *efficiency*; while improved efficiency can be a byproduct, it is not the chief purpose of maximum power transfer. It implies that although higher percentage of power is transferrable, it does not affect the magnitude of the power load (i.e. the extent that it can affect a circuit). In the event that the internal resistance is modified to accommodate a value higher than the value of the original resistance, improved efficiency can be achieved.

Moreover, the concept of maximum power transfer was initially misunderstood; a subject of many arguments was a circuit's reduced efficiency with the occurrence of transfer. Some insisted that due to the potential power that is lost during an exchange, a circuit may fail to reach 100% efficiency. As emphasis of this group's angle, take for example the case of a motor whose power is transferred from a battery; power in this situation may not be maximized, and it will only be realized over time when battery power has been fully consumed.

The maximum power theory states that the task of transferring power consumes power, too

It was *Thomas Edison*, as well as his fellow scientists, *Francis Robbins Upton*, who contested that maximum power transfer and efficiency are only *relative*; the 2 concepts are not one and the same. In fact, there is a discussion about *maximum power efficiency*, too.

In the exchange, you will find that *resistance* plays an important role. By giving light to the former argument, you can calculate a circuit's capability of a maximum power transfer, in relation to maximum power efficiency with the following formula:

MPT = RL ÷ (RL + RS)

A circuit's *MPT* (or maximum power transfer) can be determined with basic arithmetic skills. First, divide the *RL* (or Resistance Load) by the sum of the *RL* and *RS* (or Resistance Source).

V.B. – Thevenin's Theory

Thevenin's Theory, conceptualized by Hermann von Helmholtz and Leon Charles Thevenin, discusses that if a circuit follows a linear network, any point can be replaced given that it remains to carry a source for current, resistance, and voltage. Behind it, the idea is to supply an equivalent.

Originally, *Thevenin's Theory* can only be applied to circuits that operate with a DC system; since a DC system is rather simple, replacing its components with an equivalent is possible. Eventually, however, its capability to handle a load in a non-linear system was discovered; it can offer solutions for an AC system.

Moreover, the *Thevenin Theory* puts emphasis on that the average circuit can only be considered to have a linear according to a limited range; it can only be replaced by the components of with values among the range.

The Thevenin Theory follows that power dissipation can yield unique values, and can also yield identical values. However, the results can only be accomplished with the power supplied by an external resistor.

V.C. – The Star Delta Transformation

The *Star Delta Transformation* dwells on the idea that a circuit's system can change from one phase to another. For instance, if a circuit's power source is altered, its ability of carrying power from a point to the next is altered, too. Especially if there are 3 branches in a circuit's system, the power that circulates is known to form a closed loop.

The Star Delta Transformation refers to 2 kinds of circuit transformations. The first circuit transformation is a star transformation, which can be described by a "Y" formation; the second circuit transformation is a delta transformation, which can be described by a triangular pattern.

Moreover, the Star-Delta Transformation describes a 3-phase network of circuits, which can explain power transfer between these 3 networks. It enables the conversion of impedances that are connected to each other. With the theory as basis, alongside getting a clear scope for power transfer analysis, solving various concerns can be accomplished, too; the concept is applicable to different types of circuits including *series circuits, bridge-type networks, resistive circuits,* and *parallel circuits.*

The Star-Delta Transformation can be converted to the Delta-Star Transformation. From the star or Y-formation, the circuit creates a triangular network as the transition is achieved.

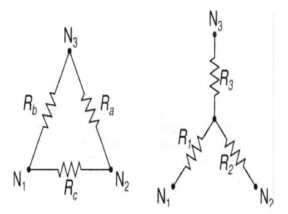

The Star-Delta Transformation or the Delta-Star Transformation is also called the Y-Δ Transformation or the Δ-Y Transformation

For the transition of the Star-Delta Transformation into the Delta-Star Transformation, a formula should be followed; this is meant to ensure that the transformation, along with the calculations for the total resistance in *all 3 circuits*, is successful. Initially, the goal is to compare the amount of power in an individual network. Once the power in network 1 has been acknowledged, proceed to identifying the weight that one network holds in the entire formation; one way of determining this is to disconnect that entire network and observe the operations of a circuit.

The formula:

**representations: $_\Delta R$ =   total resistance of the transformation

$_1N$ = resistance in node 1

$_2N$ = resistance in node 2

$_AR$ = resistance in circuit A

$_BR$ = resistance in circuit B

$_CR$ = resistance in circuit C

$_\Delta R \, (_1N \, _2N) = {_C}R \, || \, (_AR + {_B}R)$

The simple version of the formula:

**representation: TR = total resistance

$_AR$ = resistance in circuit A

$_BR$ = resistance in circuit B

$_CR$ = resistance in circuit C

$_TR = {_A}R + {_B}R + {_C}R$

V.D. – Extra Element Theory

A circuit analysis technique that can be used for the simplification of a complicated problem is *the Extra Element Theory*; it was proposed by R.D. Middlebrook. The idea behind it is to take a complex matter, then divide it into small portions; each of the small portions will be addressed.

It follows that every circuit has a *transfer function* and *driving point*; the process of analyzing a circuit, therefore, can become easier if the aforementioned elements are first identified.

In the Extra Element Theory, unlike in other circuitry theorems, an element such as a capacitor or resistor can be temporarily removed so the transfer function or driving point can be determined. Since there are circuit components that can complicate an equation (regardless of how integral they are to a circuit), it is practical to set them aside for a while; although they may be of value to a circuit as a whole, it was proven that they don't affect calculations. Once the initial goal is achieved, the elements can be returned.

Impedance is a familiar term in discussions of the Extra Element Theory; it can be analyzed with the employment of the theory. In certain cases, its input can be determined in network granted that an *extra element* joins in.

The Extra Element Theory (in relation to input impedance) proposes the addition of an "extra" element that is equivalent in value to the other elements

The formula for finding the impedance is:

**representations: Z = impedance

s = source

$Z = 1 \div s$

V.E. – Simplification of the Source

Simplification of the Source, sometimes referred to as Source Transformation, is the process of converting electric current into voltage, or voltage into electric current. It is a common technique used by many circuit engineers for explaining their circuit's system in simple terms.

The process of Simplification of the Source usually begins with an existing resistance source in a circuit; it is then replaced with new electric current source with a similar level of resistance. Since it is *bilateral procedure*, one can be derived to yield results from another. It makes way for the adjustment of voltage as it gradually becomes the equivalent of a particular circuit's resistance.

Moreover, *Simplification of the Source* may begin with an existing resistance, but is *not limited to the accommodation of resistive circuits*. It means that the process can be performed on circuits that involve inductors and capacitors.

V.F. – Where Does the Rosenstark Method Fit in?

The *Rosenstark Method*, sometimes called *Asymptotic Gain Model*, is yet another important subject where power transfer is concerned. In light of the return ratio, it serves as the representation of *negative gain* from feedback amplifiers. As it provides an intuitive form of circuit analysis, it introduces a new batch of elements such as the *return ratio* and *asymptotic gains*.

The Rosenstark formula:

**representations: G_o = 0 asymptotic gain

G_∞ = infinite asymptotic gain

T = return ratio

Rosenstark Method = $\{G_o + [T \div (T + 1)]\} + \{G_\infty + [T \div (T + 1)]\}$

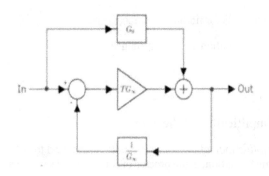

The Rosenstark Method serves as the basic representation of power transfer in a circuit

Best features of the Rosenstark Method:

- Assumes that the direct transmission is small and can be equated to the asymptotic gain

- Characterizes bilateral properties and feedback amplifiers

- Identifies (via thorough inspection) the passive circuit elements

Steps:

1. Choose a source in a circuit's system; preferably, opt for a dependent source.

2. Determine the source's return ratio.

3. Identify the G_∞.

4. Identify the G_0.

5. Use the Rosenstark formula and substitute values.

Chapter VI – Laws, Laws & More Laws

Come to think of it, *circuit analysis* is one of the broad branches of electrical engineering. It covers the basics of circuits and power consumption; it also covers the extensive aspects of the topic such as the operations of an entire electrical network.

Without laws regarding how electric current is distributed within a circuit's components, there is a risk of unclear discussions of *fundamental and in-depth analysis*; without them, a guide that can break down lengthy components is absent. For beginners, especially, they are important since they grant the chance to understand the functions of a circuit and even each one of its parts. It stays true to the idea that for the resolution of a big problem, looking at it like little pieces is an opportunity to conqueror its difficulties.

VI.A. – Putting Kirchhoff's Laws into Motion

Kirchhoff's Laws are composed of *2 equations* that dwell on the conservation of charge and energy. They were initially introduced in 1845 by Gustav Kirchhoff as a means for the determination of a circuit's power consumption, as well as its parameters.

As several discussions go, Kirchhoff's Laws may not be too important since it was derived from the work of Scottish physicist, *James Maxwell*; since it was derived from another's work, it is said that a circuit engineer should rather use the original work as basis. However, it is a set of laws that primarily focuses on the operations of a closed circuit; the previous work from which it was taken doesn't put emphasis on a closed circuit, and is rather descriptive of the generic circuit.

Moreover, Kirchoff's Laws are conditional. It may be useful in describing charge and energy conservation for different circuit elements, but it can only yield an *approximation*; it also requires certain factors such as changing electric currents, voltage, and resistance.

Kirchhoff's Law is actually a general term. To be specific, it addresses 2 subjects: current and voltage. It acknowledges all circuits, regardless of complexities.

To solidify its argument in the conservation of charge and energy, one of Kirchhoff's Laws, *KCL* (or Kirchhoff's Current Law), states that the electric current in an interconnected network is relative. And, to emphasize his point, Gustav Kirchhoff contests that the algebraic sum of the electric current in a joint network is *0*.

Another law of Kirchhoff that complements the KCL is *KVL* (or Kirchhoff's Voltage Law). Its basis is on the general law on energy conservation that defines voltage as the energy per unit of charge. Just like in the previous law, Gustav Kirchhoff says that in a closed network, the algebraic sum of the electric voltage in a joint network is *0*.

According to KVL, adding all the voltages within the circuit yields 0

VI.B. – Does Michael Faraday Know What He's Getting Into?

The *Law of Induction* by *Michael Faraday* is a fundamental law that revolves around the field of a circuit and the possible elements that are subject to eventual interaction. It carries both qualitative and quantitative aspects, and proposes that only with the presence of an infinite source of inductors can a circuit retain its inductive capability.

Unfortunately, not all circuit engineers and scientists are one with *Michael Faraday* and his *Law of Induction*. It is argued that although it holds some matters true, especially where loops of wire are concerned, it can yield the wrong results if used extensively; it can only handle a certain field and is usually arbitrarily small. In fact, counterexamples were previously presented.

A counterexample of Faraday's Law of Induction is the case involving an *electric disc generator*. Due to its own magnetic field, it can rotate circularly at a specified angular rate; it can complete a rotation and in the process, induct electricity by distributing it to other areas (within the circuit). It can be deduced that although the circuit's shape has remained constant over a period of time and although it can induct electricity, its distributive method made it lose inductive capabilities.

An electric disc generator induces electricity until cycle completion in the object's lower brush.

Faraday's Law of Induction may have been noted for certain flaws, but it is a law that made the conception of other important laws (not all of them are in the field of circuit engineering) possible. An important law with basis on Michael Faraday's idea is Albert Einstein's *Special Relativity*.

VI.C. - Ohm's Law & Conductivity

Ohm's Law, named after the German scientist, Georg Simon Ohm, is a powerful law that describes the resistance and electric current in a circuit, as well as their potential difference. Particularly, it sheds light on 2 points, then, subjects them to further analysis. Consequently, the relationship between Point A and Point B will indicate each of their properties as individual components.

In the verge of learning its concepts, it will dawn on you that *Ohm's Law* is an *empirical matter*. After observations with different ranges of length scales, it was proposed that it would fail where small wires are concerned; however, this proved to be a mere assumption since it was discovered that it could function regardless of a wire's size.

Since it is a basic equation in circuit engineering, *Ohm's Law* can also be applied for the determination of metal conductivity; it can be relied on when it comes to understanding the electric flow and conductive aspect in a circuit's component. Various materials that make use of Georg Ohm's principles are referred to as *ohmic*.

Georg Ohm set the parameters for his law to include only common terms in circuitry

In the physics of electricity, Ohm's Law is important where quantitative measurements in a circuit are concerned. Initially, when it was presented to German scientists, it was only mocked and rejected due to the mere fact that it went against the basic understanding of electric flow; it was dismissed as "a web of fancies" and worse, Georg Ohm was dubbed as a "fancy but invaluable" science professor. It was only until 1840 when it earned recognition and is now widely used today.

How to calculate for the elements in Ohm's Law:

Formula # 1:

voltage = current* resistance

Formula # 2:

current = voltage ÷ resistance

Formula # 3:

resistance = voltage ÷ current

VI.D. – The Argument of Norton's Theorem

Edward Lawry Norton, as he implies in *Norton's Theorem*, proposed that in circuit analysis, any linear network, granted that it has sources of voltage, electric current, and resistance, has an equivalent in dual network. A certain system may be unique, but values that can make a similar model can be obtained.

To find a circuit's equivalent using Norton's concepts, certain values need to be identified: voltage, electric current, and resistance. Once there are clear sources, you can begin formulating the necessary equations. However, when the sources are dependent on each other, another (and it has to be from a generic source) electric current needs to enter the picture.

Moreover, Norton's Theorem gives light to the fact that the values for the *equivalent current* and *equivalent voltage* are values that can be identified at the first 2 terminals of a circuit. It is important to note, however, that such a case is only possible if all the components in the said circuit are *short-circuited*. If the components are not short-circuited, a practical solution is to have current and voltage sources replaced; current can be replaced by transforming a circuit into an open circuit, and voltage can be replaced by transforming a circuit into a short circuit.

Norton's Theorem was also developed by Hands Ferdinand Mayer

The formula:

**representations: TC_{AB} = total current in circuit A and circuit B

TC = total current

TC_{AB} = voltage ÷ (TC in circuit A + TC in circuit B)

VI.E. – Coulomb's Law

One of the laws that underwent heavy testing is a law that gives importance to the electrostatic relationship of all the charged elements within a circuit; this law is called *Coulomb's Law* after the scientist, Charles Agustin de Coulomb. It argues that the magnitude of interactive circuit components is in direct proportion to the *squared area* between the distances. To demonstrate a point, it shows that the primary force works along a straight line.

Moreover, Coulomb's Law requires that the placement of the charged elements is accomplished through a single medium. This causes the arrangement to eliminate any possible complications.

The application of Coulomb's Law is only valid if the circuit components are point charges

To make it effortless to obey Coulomb's Law, the determination of *Coulomb's constant* is recommended. Once the value of the constant has been determined, not only is it easier to adhere to the aforementioned law, you are also ensuring that the calculations for the electric current are valid.

The formula:

**representations: CC = Coulomb's Constant

ε_o = electric constant

$CC = 1 \div 4\pi \times \varepsilon_o$

Chapter VII – Understanding Electromagnetism

A pair of loudspeakers is an example of an electronic device that works due to the *strategic positioning* of circuit elements. That, along with the integral parts called *electromagnets*; such components cause disturbance to other circuit elements. Their effect on their fellows is rather significant as they tend to make the device's cone to vibrate. As a result, sound, and in most cases, high quality sound, is produced.

For a deeper understanding of a loudspeaker, you could use a lesson in *electromagnetism.*

VII.A. – An Introduction to the Concept behind Electromagnetism

Electromagnetism is a branch of science that involves the study of electricity and magnetism. It follows that wherever there is an electric field, there is also a magnetic field. It was initially introduced and developed by *Hans Christian Orsted.* In 1802, an Italian scholar by the name of *Gian Domenico Romagnosi* also examined the field

In circuitry, understanding the concept behind electromagnetism is important due the possibly strong electromagnetic reaction of circuit components. It follows that the *EMF* (or electromagnetic force) of any circuit serves a major role in the determination of internal properties.

Chapter V, *Power Transfer at Max*, and Chapter VI, *Laws, Laws & More Laws,* contain different discussions about transferring electric current and voltage. In electromagnetism, more discussions about transfer will be tackled. This time, however, the focus is on the charged elements in a circuit (whether negatively or positively charged), as well as their responses when exposed to movement.

The primary principles of electromagnetism:

- The direction of a magnetic field dictates the direction of the current in a circuit

- The electric current of a conductor creates a magnetic field; the formation is dependent on the direction of the conductor, but is always shaped in a corresponding circle

- The magnetic poles of charged elements always come in pairs; one pole in a pair needs to be inversely proportional to the other

- Charged elements can either attract or repel; elements with different charges are attractive to each other, while those with similar charges avoid contact

- Electric current can be induced when it is moved away or toward a magnetic field

VII.B. – Gauss Who?

A notable individual in the field of electromagnetism is *Carl Friedrich Gauss*. He is a German mathematician who put together the critical electromagnetism concepts in the form of a law called *Gauss Law*. According to him, to determine the relevance of the distribution of electric charges, the circuit's electric field, in its entirety, must be evaluated.

Gauss Law allows mathematical expression with the employment of *integral* and *differential calculus*, preferably in vector form. For a beginner in circuitry, the particular technique of demonstration is advised since it grants a clear perspective of the concept of electromagnetism.

The integral formula:

**representations: Φ_E = electric field

ε_0 = electric constant

Q = total electric charge

$$\Phi_E = Q \div \varepsilon_0$$

The differential formula:

**representations: ∇ = an electric field's divergence

E = the other half of an electric field's divergence

p = electric charge density

ε_0 = electric constant

$$\nabla \times E = p \div \varepsilon_0$$

VII.C. – The Main Formulas in Electromagnetism

In a circuit's electromagnetic field, it is important to remember that charged elements tend to move radically; sometimes, predicting the direction of the electric flow is nearly impossible. While others go about in a non-linear network, many charges obey the rule of superposition since they adhere to a linear path. With the use of certain laws as basis, the relationship between the charged elements can be evaluated.

4 laws:

1. Ampere's Law – an important law whose applications include instances of a moving magnetic field; particularly, it be applied in situations involving current-carrying wires

   The formula:

   **representations: B = electromagnetic field

   DL = differential element of the electric current

   $\mu 0$ = permeability of 0 space

   I = electric current in an enclosed circuit

   $\int B \, X \, DL = \mu 0 \, X \, I$

2. Biot-Savart's Law – a law that is employed for the calculation of steady current in an electromagnetic field; a requirement is a constant time variable, as well as a charge that is a subject of neither a build-up or depletion

   The formula:

   **representations: B = electromagnetic field outside a circuit

   $\mu 0$ = permeability of 0 space

   I = electric current in an enclosed circuit

   R = distance from the electromagnetic field

   $B = \int (\mu 0 \, X \, I) \div 4\pi \, R^2$

3. Faraday's Law – like his [Michael Faraday] law of induction, this is a law that addresses the induced electromagnetic force of an object; it is strictly applicable to the charged elements within a closed circuit

   The formula:

   **representations: IEMF = induced electromagnetic field

   $D\varphi$ = difference of space

   DT = time differential

   $IEMF = - \, D\varphi \div DT$

4. Lorentz Force – a law that assesses a point charge due to both an electromagnetic field and an electric field

   The formula:

**representations: LF = Lorentz Force

q = total charge

EMF = electromagnetic field inside a circuit

V = velocity

B = electromagnetic field outside a circuit

LF = q [EMF + (V X B)]

VII.D. – Electrodynamics & Quantum Electrodynamics

Before the 1900s, a scientist named William Gilbert addressed a proposal concerning *electricity* and *magnetism*; according to him, while both subjects can be traced to attracting and repulsing objects within a circuit, electricity and magnetism are different concepts. The key to understanding electromagnetism, therefore, is to understand the individual terms; particularly, understand their relevance and distinction.

A conflict regarding electromagnetism is that, despite agreeing to Albert Einstein's *Special Relativity*, it goes against some of the rules of mechanics; it is only dependent on the electromagnetic permeability of 0 space. It follows that in the case of moving frames, the electromagnetic field is subjected to transformation to include space.

Moreover, all electromagnetic phenomena are covered under *quantum mechanics*. This makes the electromagnetic field of a circuit accountable for the physical phenomena that are observable, especially *magnetism* and *electricity*.

Chapter VIII – Let's Talk Circuit Boards

Are you familiar with *crocodile clips?*

Crocodile clips are devices that can be used for the assembly of a circuit; these tools are so-named for their resemblance to the jaws of a crocodile. With them, a solid grip to connect a component is possible. If you're wondering how electrical engineers can create electrical connections without the associated dangers? Well, there's your answer.

By using *crocodile clips*, you can make a model of a working circuit. Whether be it a basic circuit, a series circuit, or a parallel circuit, you can create for an audience to analyze.

VIII.A. - Printed Circuit Boards 101

Printed circuit boards (or PCBs) are devices that enable electrical connectivity even in an "open" environment; within their system, there are resistors, inductors, transformers, capacitors, conductors, and semi-conductors. These tools support high component density. In a way, printed circuit boards are referred to as *live circuits.*

Since functioning circuit boards can be rather risky, especially when exposed to extreme environments, they are packaged accordingly. In most cases, these devices are subjected to a series of coating procedures and are dipped in acrylic, wax, polyurethane, and epoxy.

Design standards:

- Templates and card dimensions are designed according to required circuitry regulations

- Manufactured Gerber data are generated

- Design is planned thoroughly with the assistance of an *EDA or Electronic Design Automation* tool

- Traces for signals are routed

- Copper thickness and layer thickness are carefully evaluated

VIII.B. – Circuit Board Tests

To see if a circuit works, certain tests are performed. Particularly, it is determined whether or not it is functional and can perform desired tasks. Along with its capacitors, resistors, transformers, and other components, it is analyzed for opens and shorts.

Objectives of testing methods:

- To detect flaws

- To detect error-free operations of each of its components

- To determine system stability

- To evaluate whether it is fit for use

- To evaluate safety issues

- To verify test systems

Example testing methods:

- Analog tests

- Contact tests

- Contact tests

- Electrolytic capacitor tests

- Flash tests

- Powered digital tests

- Short tests

VIII.C. – Let's Learn to Prototype

Prototyping is the ability to put a particular idea to test by preparing a model from which other circuits are developed. Especially when the circuit in subject involves a complex system or expensive components, a prototype is initially designed.

If the circuit creator is unsure of how a particular circuit will function, his best bet is to create a *prototype*. This way, he can evaluate his creation and see how it can be improved. If it's not yielding his desired results, he can modify the placements of each of its components until he achieves a necessary output. Otherwise, he can proceed to the actual circuit-making process.

VIII.D. - The Art of Bread-Boarding

Breadboards allow the creation of a circuit prototype, which is the reason why these tools are ideal for beginners. *Bread-boarding*, therefore, is the process of creating a circuit prototype in a board to resemble the operations of a real circuit. Its history can be traced to the time that electrical enthusiasts would use a literal breadboard (i.e. the board used for slicing bread).

According to experts, it's recommended to learn and understand bread-boarding prior to making your first-ever circuit. It's advised to be familiar with each of its components, as well as how it works.

Breadboard components:

- Chips – these are *legs* that come out of both sides of a breadboards; these components fit perfectly and serve as connectors of different parts

- Posts – these are components that enable connections from power sources

- Power rails – these are vertical metal rows strips that are adjacent to terminals; through these components, easy access to a power source can be provided

- Power supplies – these are components that enable the supplementation of a wide range of electric current and voltage levels

- Terminals – these are horizontal metal row strips that are adjacent to power rails; through these components, wires are allowed to be inserted, then, be held intact

VIII.E. – Essential Skills in Circuitry

After understanding *bread-boarding*, you're almost ready for some hands-on circuit lessons. First, however, you should adopt a certain set of skills; while bread-boarding is helpful, it's only practice (i.e. for instance, there is no soldering involved). Since you'll be making an actual functioning circuit, it's time to get your hands dirty.

5 skills required in circuitry:

1. Stripping (wire) – it is a skill that promotes secure electrical connections; it involves the knowledge on various types of wires, thickness of wires, and how to maintain a solid grip; since exposure to electric current is a risk, it is best to check out the appropriate tools for wires

2. Drilling – it is a skill that focuses on the proper drilling (of holes) in a circuit, then, making sure that electrical connections can remain intact; it is a slow process that requires practice with accuracy and precision

3. How to test batteries – it is a skill that requires testing the capacity of a battery; particularly, it involves measuring the current load in open and short circuits

4. How to use a glue gun – it is a skill that takes advantage of a glue gun's conductive property; it teaches how to insulate and how to set a semi-permanent coating; especially when there is a need to strengthen the joints of a circuit, it comes in handy

5. How to use liquid electrical coating – it is a skill that focuses on the ability to apply liquid electrical coating where conventional electrical tape is likely to fail; it requires precaution since about 30% of the parts in the liquid coating are quite volatile

VIII.F. – The Secrets of a Solder

Soldering is a process that involves (at least) 2 metals (or any conductive material); the 2 metals are joined by flowing and melting. In the industry of circuitry, it is one of the most fundamental methods in circuit creation; it allows independent components to work as one.

A technique of good soldering revolves around the knowledge of the amount of heat that is applied. For *basic soldering, 361F* is the temperature to consider and for *advanced soldering*, the goal is to arrive at a temperature of somewhere between *361F to 419F*.

In *metallurgical engineering*, a term named *flux* is commonly used; in circuit engineering, as soon as the circuit creation process commences, it will be introduced, too. It is cleaning agent and a flowing material that facilitates the soldering process. Should there be invisible impurities (e.g. oil, dirt, etc.), they will be removed for the purpose of not risking the integrity of a circuit.

Moreover, it is important to note that in soldering, the proper application of flux is suggested. Improper methods can result to joint failure. The system's damage (due to incorrect flux application) may not be obvious at first, but gradually, it is capable of corrosion and rendering a circuit useless.

Chapter IX – Sufficient Safety

On a sunny day, try heading outside of your house, then, checking out the electrical connections (wires) from one post to another. More likely, one, two, or even a flock of birds are calmly resting on power lines.

Do you ever wonder why they don't get shocked?

No, birds are normal creatures; they do not possess extra-special powers. In their heads, they understand that it's a must not to step on open electrical networks, which is one of the things that need to be covered for beginners in circuit engineering.

IX.A. – The Lack of Electrical Safety Courses

While some *circuit engineering professors* teach enough lessons about *electrical safety*, others are quite behind on the area. They assume that practical knowledge, as well as a general "be careful" would suffice; since the beginners in circuit engineering are frequent exposure to electrical devices, no, the statement won't cut it. Therefore, it is important to stress out the need to be careful especially during their first hands-on activity.

Electrical safety tips:

- Treat each electrical device as if live current is running inside it (regardless if you're aware that there isn't)

- Overloading sockets for a circuit board? Not a good idea

- To cut off running current, add a residual current

- Always disconnect (and not just turn off) electrical devices when working on a component

- Always turn off any electrical device if not in use

- Regularly check the conditions of sockets and plugs

- Practice extreme caution when dealing with liquids and electric current

- Make sure your hands are dry

- Avoid octopus connections (i.e. devices that enable multiple plugs or sockets)

- Keep electrical wires and cords tucked neatly

- Wear the proper attire when creating a circuit; put on non-conductive gloves and footwear with insulated soles

IX.B. - The Importance of Hands-on Circuit Lessons

Hands-on learning is important for a beginner in circuits. It gives light to the fact that in circuit engineering, it is more about actual field work. Once the concepts are understood, it's best to move on to creating functional circuit boards.

A common problem that is encountered by beginners? Sweaty hands. Even in an air-conditioned laboratory, there are people who have to deal with sweaty hands when handling circuits. Alongside, they have to deal with the need of maintaining a strong and solid grip on various tools. Although this may be a concern, it's one that requires practice.

IX.C. – The 80-20 Rule of Circuit Safety

In circuitry, there is a rule that focuses on the installments of transmitters in hazardous areas for devices with a circuit; it is called the *80-20 Rule of Circuit Safety*. According to the rule, it is recommended to take extra precaution when dealing with particular portions of an electronic device; there are some parts that increase the risk of electrical shock when *touched* or *moved*.

Hazardous areas of a circuit (that require extra precaution):

- Point with high impedance

- Point with high resistance

- Area near the voltage source

- Area near an opening

- Area with conductive elements

IX.D. – Troubleshooting Concerns

In the event that a device with a circuit is not function correctly, it is recommended to have it evaluated accordingly. While a beginner may handle the task of checking, a professional in circuitry is the one who is advised to assess the system. Since an expert is already familiar with different circuit components, and he knows exactly where to look for possible faults, he is more qualified for the job.

Troubleshooting tips:

- Determine whether the connections are secure

- Determine whether the wires are correctly connected to one
  another

- Check for circuit components that seem out of place

- Check for circuit components that may be larger in size

Chapter X – Here's a Multimeter for You!

An important and indispensible tool in circuitry is a *multimeter*.

Imagine a situation when a circuit project was presented to you. Since you were requested to detail accurate measurements for its electric current, voltage, and resistance, you go to the nearest equipment laboratory to borrow a stack of devices for assistance.

Now, imagine the same situation, but this time, you have this tool; instead of having to go to the equipment laboratory to borrow a stack of devices to measure the electric current, voltage, and resistance, you turn to that tool. This particular time, you have a multimeter.

If you're not familiar with the operations of a multimeter, let it be your first job prior to creating a circuit project. It's actually quite easy to use. So long as you are attentive to instructions, and you know its components, certain restriction, and the technique to maximizing its functions, you're set.

X.A. - What's a Multimeter?

A multimeter, also called a multitester, *Volt-Ohm millimeter*, and *Volt-Ohm meter*, is an electronic device that measures the electric current in a circuit; it is capable of measuring voltage, resistance, and a variety of other units in a circuit's system. To know how to use the device, it's important to be familiar with each of its components; if you can understand how the components work, you can also understand the operations of the entire device.

Parts of a multimeter:

1. The selection knob – it enables a user to choose a particular setting that is subject for measurement

2. The display meter – it enables the display of the measured reading; it can contain up to 4 digits, as well as a negative sign

3. The probes – these are plugged into a multimeter that can interpret and convert measurements from a device into a multimeter; usually, these come in a pair of red and black probes

   Types of probes:

   I.   IC hook

   II.   Alligator clips

   III.   Test probes

X.B. - A Multimeter in the Works

Inarguably, a multimeter is one of the most useful tools in circuitry and one of the tools that can make the task of building circuits easy. It can be used to measure *any object or device* that contains a circuit and an electric current. Using it, however, comes the hard part; in fact, in the world of circuits and electronics, it earned the title as one of the most challenging jobs. It may be effortless to get a reading, but getting an accurate reading, then interpreting the reading is another story.

How to use a multimeter to measure (a basic example):

1. Prepare an AAA battery.

2. Plug the black probe of a multimeter to the negative side (i.e. the side with a "-") of the AAA battery.

3. Plug the red probe of a multimeter to the positive side of the AAA battery.

4. Check the display meter; as recommended, check the meter twice.

5. List down the reading and begin the interpretation.

X.C. – Resolution, Accuracy & Input Impedance

The smallest part of a multimeter's scale is called as the *resolution*. It is responsible for achieving an accurate reading and interpretation. In many multimeter kinds, especially digital ones, it can be configured or *calibrated*. And, as the rules go, a device with low resolution doesn't require much completion time; a device with high resolution can require a demanding processing time.

Meanwhile, the *accuracy* of a multimeter refers to an error in the measurement of an electric current, in comparison to a perfect reading. It is relative to the device's resolution since resolution may not be calibrated accordingly if the absolute accuracy level is questionable. Therefore, to determine the total accuracy of a multimeter, its relative accuracy should be added to its absolute accuracy.

Formula for the computation of total accuracy:

**representations: TA = total accuracy

RA = relative accuracy

AA = absolute accuracy

$TA = RA + AA$

When talking about a multimeter's resolution and accuracy, *input impedance* is a set of terms that needs to be acknowledged, too. This is due to the device's inability to achieve accurate readings when it is not set accordingly. Especially for the measurement of a circuit's voltage, its input impedance has to be calibrated high (i.e. higher than a circuit's voltage) so the operation remains smoothly.

X.D. – Safety Concerns

Groups that are in charge of the manufacture of multimeters, as well as the authorities that promote the safe use of such devices have set safety standards. This is to emphasize the importance of the right employment of the electrical tools. Although the method for use can be rather straightforward, reckless habits can result to problems. Alongside the possibility of inaccurate readings, it can cause harm to the individual that is handling the devices.

Categories of safety standards:

- Category 1 – applicable to the employment of a multimeter, circuit, or any electronic equipment with a distance near main connections

- Category 2 – applicable to the employment of a multimeter, circuit, or any electronic equipment with a distance somewhere near the first phase of main connections

- Category 3 –applicable to the employment of a multimeter, circuit, or any electronic equipment with a distance near permanently installed loads

- Category 4 – applicable to the employment of a multimeter, circuit, or any electronic equipment with a distance near faulty current levels that can be quite high

Chapter XI - DIY Circuits: Simple Projects

When you're into circuits, as well as *electronics and electrical engineering*, you need to step up your game when it comes to building items. Isn't the main reason for learning the branch of electrical engineering for the creation of circuits, then, putting them to good use?

In the event that your first circuit project wouldn't turn out as desired, try not to get discouraged easily, and instead, give matters another go. Not getting the results you wanted maybe a bit of a downer, but eventually, the odds will be in your favor; look at the setback as an opportunity for learning. If your heart's into circuits, you'll soon get the hang of how things are done.

XI.A. – Common Tools in Circuitry

For the creation of a circuit, you can make use of just about any tool you come across; if you find equipment that will make you accomplish a task easier, then, maybe you should put it in your arsenal. You *can* use just any tool, yes, but, doing so is not advised. It is best to choose the right set (i.e. a set of tools with a non-conductive handle) to not put your safety at risk.

Common tools:

- Crimper

- Cutters (e.g. cable cutter, electrical cutter, etc.)

- Extraction tool

- Glue gun

- Non-metallic tweezers

- Pliers

- Screwdriver

- Soldering gun

- Wire-wrapping tools

XI.B. - Beginner Circuit Projects

Building your first circuit can be a challenge; since you're still a beginner, you may end up making mistakes. Maybe your circuit won't end up as functional as desired, despite having followed your understanding of a series of procedures. In such a case, this is where you have to tweak your work; be diligent in figuring out where you went wrong. If you're uncertain of your actions' impact, don't worry too much. The important part is to begin; you can, then, figure out the rest along the way.

7 easy circuit projects (derived from http://www.instructables.com):

- Project # 1 – Static Electricity Analyzer

    The Static Electricity Analyzer can detect nearby static electricity; to indicate that static electricity is present, its LED component glows. Apart from a detector, it can be used to analyze the electricity in its surroundings. It is an extremely sensitive device since it can even detect nearby hand movement without touching the antenna.

    Materials:

    - Around 10 pieces wire

    - 1 piece LED

    - 1 piece static electricity antenna

    - 1 piece 100K resistor

    - 1 piece 1M resistor

    - 3 pieces 2n222 transistor

    Procedures (as shown in the layout above):

    1. To the left side of the circuit board, connect the 1M resistor to 2n222 transistor.

    2. Beside it, attach the wire, then, attach the static electricity antenna.

3. On the bottom, attach the wire, then, attach the other 2n222 transistor; next to it, attach the wire, and finally, attach the third 2n222 transistor.

4. Place the 100K resistor adjacent to the second 2n222 transistor.

5. Place the LED adjacent to the third 2n222 resistor.

6. Establish connection to a power supply.

- Project # 2 – Dark LED Light

The Dark LED Light is a circuit project that can detect darkness. It follows that when insufficient light is supplied, an IC timer is alerted; consequently, a high output is produced and LED light will be switched on. The idea behind it is similar to that of a street light that automatically turns on once it detects that it's already evening.

Materials:

- Around 10 pieces wire

- 1 piece LED

- 1 piece LDR

- 1 piece 10nf capacitor

- 1 piece 100nf capacitor

- 1 piece 10K resistor

- 1 piece 100K resistor

- 1 piece 555 IC timer

Procedures (as shown in the layout above):

1. On top of the LDR, attach the 100K resistor.

2. On the bottom of the LDR, create a connection to the LED.

3. To the left of the LED, create a connection to the 10nf capacitor.

4. To the left of the 10nf capacitor, create a connection to the 100nf capacitor.

5. Next to the 100nf capacitor, create a connection to the 10K resistor.

6. Place the 555 IC timer between all the connections; establish the main connection by attaching the other ends of the LED, LDR, capacitors, and resistors to the 555 IC timer (directly or with a wire).

7. Establish connection to a power supply.

- Project # 3 – The Ticking Bomb

The Ticking Bomb is meant for creating a ticking sound that resembles a bomb. Once it is turned on, it produces sound that is adjustable, but is modified to 1 tick per second.

Materials:

- Around 10 pieces wire

- 2 pieces 10uf capacitors

- 1 piece 555 IC timer

- 1 piece 47K resistor

- 1 piece 8 ohm speaker

Procedures (as shown in the layout above):

1. Make the 555 IC timer as the central component; to its left, create a connection to the 47K resistor.

2. On the bottom, create a connection to the first 10uf capacitor; then, create a connection from the 10uf capacitor to the 47K resistor.

3. To the right of the 555 IC timer, create a connection to the second 10uf capacitor.

4. From the second 10uf capacitor, create a connection to the 8 ohm speaker.

5. Establish connection to a power supply.

- Project # 4 – The Remote Tester

The Remote Tester, as its name suggests, is a circuit that checks whether or not a remote control is working. Behind it, the idea is focused on the sufficient amount of signals that the IR receiver is getting. If it receives enough signals, the LED lights up, which means that a particular remote control is functioning; conversely, if the LED remains as is, it is an indication of a faulty component in the device.

Materials:

- Around 10 pieces wire

- 1 piece LED

- 1 piece IR receiver

- 1 piece 1K resistor

- 1 piece bc557 transistor

- 1 piece 10uf capacitor

Procedures (as shown in the layout above):

1. On top of the bc557 transistor, create a connection to the LED.

2. Adjacent of the bc557 transistor (to the left), create a direct path to the 1K resistor, then, to the IR receiver.

3. On the bottom, create a connection to the 10uf capacitor.

4. Connect the 10uf capacitor (directly or with wire) to close the connection.

5. Establish connection to a power supply.

- Project # 5 – The Bell Experiment

The Bell Experiment is a basic project that produces a musical sound; the result is a device that may be similar to a doorbell. It works according to each of its components; if the resistor, transistor, and IC are triggered, the bunch sends a signal to the speaker, which will then, create the sound.

Materials:

- Around 10 pieces wire

- 1 piece 1K resistor

- 1 piece 2n222 transistor

- 1 piece UM66 IC

- 1 piece 8 ohm speaker

Procedures (as shown in the layout above):

1. On one end of the 8 ohm speaker, create a connection to the 2n222 transistor.

2. On another end, create a connection to the 1K resistor.

3. From the 1K resistor, create a connection to the UM66 IC; make sure that the UM66 is parallel to the 8 ohm speaker.

4. Connect the UM66 (directly or with wire) to the 2n222 transistor to close the circuit.

5. Establish connection to a power supply.

- Project # 6 – The LED That Fades

The LED That Fades is a project that produces and sometimes, blinking lights. It operates according to the weakness or strength of the signals that are interpreted by each of its components. If its IC timer, transistor, resistor, and capacitor receive strong signals; the LED will glow; conversely, if they receive weak signals, the light starts to fade. In the event that the signals that are submitted are unstable (i.e. they alternate between weak or strong in a few minutes' time), the blinking pattern comes in.

Materials:

- Around 10 pieces wire

- 1 piece LED

- 1 piece 555 IC timer

- 1 piece bc547 transistor

- 1 piece 33K resistor

- 1 piece 220 ohm resistor

- 1 piece 100uf capacitor

Procedures (as shown in the layout above):

1. To the bottom of the bc547 transistor, create a connection to the LED.

2. Parallel to the LED, create a connection to the 100uf capacitor.

3. On top of the 100uf 33K resistor, create a connection to the 220 ohm resistor.

4. Next to the 220 ohm resistor, create a connection to the 555 IC timer.

5. Create a connection around the 555 IC timer for a closed circuit.

6. Establish connection to a power supply.

- Project # 7 – The LED with Activated Light

The LED with Activated Light is a basic project for beginners in circuit engineering; it is meant for a clearer understanding of the concept of resistance. The LED lights up with the application of sufficient resistance; if resistance levels are insufficient, the light won't be activated.

Materials:

- Around 10 pieces wire

- 1 piece LED

- 1 piece LDR

- 1 piece 10nf capacitor

- 1 piece 100nf capacitor

- 1 piece 10K resistor

- 1 piece 4.7K resistor

- 1 piece 555 IC timer

- 1 piece 220 ohm resistor

Procedures (as shown in the layout above):

1. To the bottom of the LDR, create a connection to the 4.7K resistor.

2. Parallel to the 4.7K resistor connection, create a new connection to the LED, followed by the 22 ohm resistor on top.

3. From the 22 ohm resistor, create a connection to the 555 IC timer.

4. To the bottom of the 555 IC timer, and parallel to the LED connection, create a new connection to the 10nf capacitor.

5. To the left of the 10nf capacitor, create a connection to the 100nf capacitor.

6. On top of the 100nf capacitor, create a connection to the 10K resistor.

7. Create a connection to close the circuit.

8. Establish connection to a power supply.

Chapter XII – Making Your Way to Circuit Design: PCB Layouts & Schematic Diagrams

If you are familiar with each of its components, you may have a good grasp of how an electronic circuit works; granted that the integral parts (e.g. power source, conductor, resistor, diode, etc.) are in place, and you were introduced to different techniques on establishing connections properly, there's a high chance that any circuit project you take on can be a success. Once an opening for a power source is identified, and the stability of an arrangement for the rest in a series is achieved, you're set.

However, if given the opportunity to make a particular circuit more functional, wouldn't you take it? Instead of settling for a random circuit design, why not have it modified for superior performance?

XII.A. - Circuit Design 101

Ever wonder why circuit engineers are paid highly and (depending on their chosen career path) are presented different career advancement opportunities (e.g. work as computer engineers, robotics specialists jobs, etc.)?

The responsibilities of circuit engineers are rather demanding; they need to be mentally tough and be open to different challenges. They spend hours and hours racking their brains out to determine how systems can be made more efficient. Chances are, there's always a way; it's up to them to look for one. When a particular project asks for it, it's mandatory for them to let their creative juices flow to arrive at a compatible solution. Otherwise, their built circuits may stop functioning eventually.

As mentioned, it's practical to design a circuit accordingly; especially with their employment for the fields of *communication, navigation, telecommunication, travel*, and other industries, their designs should consider a particular purpose. Apart from the objective of meeting different requirements, there needs to be a strategy since a more functional circuit comes with higher quality; it can make a project consume a reduced number of resources, too.

Reasons why there are various circuit designs:

- Improvement of a circuit's efficiency

- Improvement of a circuit's size and weight

- Guarantee a circuit's durability for a set period

- Guarantee a circuit is safe to use

XII.B. – The Design Process

Many times, a PCB layout (as discussed in chapter VII, *Let's Talk about Circuit Boards*) and a schematic diagram are often interchanged in circuitry; it has led others, especially the novices in circuit engineering, to believe that they are one and the same. In a way, since they are both presentations of a circuit's system, they may seem similar. However, upon closer inspection, they are not. It is, therefore, essential in the circuit design process that the difference is acknowledged.

A *PCB layout* is a physical representation or a *real model* of a circuit. It presents all of the electrical components that are included; it also details which of the components are active and which ones are passive. Although it can show an actual working circuit, understanding the functions of each of its parts can be tedious.

A PCB layout is an actual circuit model

On the other hand, a *schematic diagram,* also called simply as a circuit diagram, is a descriptive outline of a circuit's system; it is the standard and less costly way of circuit representation. It is like a PCB layout that shows both of the active and passive components in a circuit; unlike a PCB layout, however, its presentations can be easily understood.

A schematic diagram can include important notes for the improvement of a circuit's design

Stages of circuit design:

- Meeting specific requirements

- The creation of a circuit diagram

- Building a breadboard, or a PCB layout

- The presentation of each circuit component (for professional evaluation)

- Applying the results of evaluation

- Testing (and retesting)

- Getting approval from professionals

Circuit design tips for beginners (preparation process):

- Categorize the components

- Construct a PCB layout, as well as a schematic diagram

- Determine the compatibility of each circuit component

Circuit design tips for beginners (circuit-building process):

- Always avoid cold solder joints

- Always separate power controls and other connections

- Always separate analog and digital components

- Create traces should hard-to-find components be included

- Remember to always make integral nodes accessible

- Solder the components systematically; solder small components first, then, solder larger components next

- Strategize the spaces you allow between components

- Take note of any heat spots

XII.C. - Circuit Symbols

On the process of building a circuit and modifying its design, an understanding of different circuit symbols is important. Descriptions of circuit components can be put in simple words; it is called a *verbal description*. However, since a thorough approach is recommended in many circuitry lessons, a visual representation can enable you to understand the electric flow in a circuit.

Here's a good comparison:

Verbal description	Visual representation
Circuit # 1 contains a light bulb, as well as D-cell battery as power source.	

Moreover, circuit symbols for a visual representation of a circuit is preferred over a verbal descriptions since they may be less complicated to understand. Especially if the particular circuit is quite advanced, a description containing words can be challenging to use as basis. If a visual model is employed, however, you can simply focus on connections, instead of the interpretation of a worded description; there is a better chance of building an impressive circuit design successfully. Especially if you have plans of advancing your place in circuit engineering by soon moving forward from a novice to a circuit expert, *memorizing* the different circuit symbols is a must.

List of basic symbols:

Symbol name	Symbol
AC	
DC	
Capacitor	
Resistor	
Fuse	
Diode	
LED	
Regulator	
Transistor	

List of basic capacitor variation symbols:

-

-

-

List of basic diode variation symbols:

-

Anode Cathode

•

Anode Cathode

•

Anode Cathode

•

List of basic switches variation symbols:

L1

COM

L2

•

•

•

List of basic transistor variation symbols:

•

•

-

XII.D. – Factors to Consider

A strategic circuit design is important since a circuit may not function at all in the absence of a good plan; if the placement of each of its components wasn't accomplished according, you may have just wasted resources. You may have the correct components but if they are not designed properly, a circuit is far from working. Besides, at the realization that you may not be design a circuit's system according to requirements, you wouldn't want to put the circuit-building project to an end at the middle of the process, right?

Moreover, the proper design structure of a circuit needs to be prioritized. Regardless if it is not meant to impress another, it should still be designed accordingly as to be a stepping stone in the possibility of handling more projects eventually. With the knowledge of how to design a circuit properly as a beginner comes the effortless knowledge on the construction of more advanced circuits eventually.

What to keep in mind:

- Time availability (of the creator) – although it can be completed quickly, a circuit project shouldn't be rushed; the project creator should be available for a set period so he can concentrate properly on a circuit. Especially if he has hardly any time to spare, it's suggested that he either determines a way to find additional time, or takes on a different project

- Difficulty level – the assessment of a circuit project is important prior to acceptance. While there are simple ones, some projects are rather complicated. If a creator is certain that he can't follow through the procedures of a particular project, he may want to consider other undertakings

- Total cost of the project – one reason that the creation of a schematic diagram and other preparations are suggested (prior to taking on a circuit project) is due to practicality regarding the overall expenses. As much as possible, the creator should consider his ability to fund a project. Especially if he plans on using expensive circuit components, he needs to think about whether he can afford the project until completion.

- The desired function – identify the reason why you took on the project. Is it for experimentation and personal use? Or, was it a request from a company? Especially if the purpose is for a commercial company, design a circuit to achieve first-rate quality.

XII.E. - Documentation, Verification & Testing

A primary benefit of the *documentation* process is its advantage of letting you identify possible errors in putting together a circuit. If you weren't successful at the end stage of your project, you can figure out exactly where you went wrong; in favor of having to disregard your current progress and starting from scratch the second time around, you can simply have certain methods modified (for improvement).

Verification, as defined in circuitry, is the process of thoroughly evaluating each of a circuit's components, as well as each of the stages in the making. The objective is to determine whether the process has been adhered to correctly. Usually, this can be a time-consuming process, but since it is intend to ensure quality, it is an important one.

In a way, the real-world version of the verification process is *testing*. Prior to a circuit's launch and its exposure to different commercial industries, it is tested in research laboratories. Like verification, it can also be a time-consuming process, and since it is the last process before a circuit is passed on to another source, it can be a labor-intensive series.

Chapter XIII – A Way Is through EDA

Are you familiar with *FABS* or *Semi-conductor fabrication facilities?*

FABS are places where circuit designs, even complex ones, can be put together; they are usually extensive since they are meant to accommodate bulk circuit projects. Inside them are various equipment for *EDA*, which is why circuit-production is rapid.

With the productivity level of FABS, semi-conductors are continuously becoming popular. And, since semi-conductors are components in a circuit, circuits grew in popularity, too.

XIII.A. - What Is EDA?

EDA, also known as *Electronic Design Automation* is a class of software equipment especially for designing a circuit or different electronic devices. It is categorized along with other modern tools used in circuitry; it eliminates the need to design a circuit by hand, which minimizes simple and critical errors, repair glitches, and suggest possible improvements.

Moreover, it's due to EDA that circuit creation and circuit production became faster. If you're concerned regarding the quality since the process is done in an automated fashion, be confident that each design underwent thorough analysis. Remember, the software equipment's design was specifically meant to address a circuit's system.

XIII.B. – Design Flows

In the world of circuitry, it's important to be informed of the concepts of EDA; it privileges a circuit creator with a good grasp of the proper way to build circuits. The employees of grand electronics companies such as *Intel, Hewlett Packard,* and *Valid Logic Systems* are all trained to have impressive knowledge of the tools, despite already having gone through years of education.

Through the years, EDA tools have undergone continuous development. Initially, the concepts were rather limited; in the *Age of EDA Invention,* the focus was merely on *routing, logic synthesis, static analysis,* and *placement.* Eventually, in the *Age of EDA Implementation,* these concepts were subjected to major improvements; more *sophisticated and advanced algorithm* for the EDA tools were considered. Come the *Age of EDA Integration,* they were further studied and were designed to cater to integrated environments.

Now, you may be wondering why there is a need to build circuits manually when there are EDA tools. Well, although the process can be accomplished easier and faster, sometimes, bringing the expertise of a circuit engineer on the table is recommended; this way, he can thoroughly evaluate the quality of a circuit's system.

Additionally, the operators of EDA tools are selected carefully; usually, they are the ones with a background in the operations of EDA tools and similar equipment. This is due to the expenses, as well as the possible complications, involved in using such devices. In the event that a need for troubleshooting arises, it's best to have somebody who is knowledgeable in circuit designs on standby.

Primary focuses of EDA:

- The presentation of schematic-driven layout

- Advanced and logical interpretation of each circuit component

- Hardware and transistor simulation

XIII.C. - Circuit-Level Optimization

The circuit-level optimization or *power optimization* of EDA tools refers to the various techniques that are employed for the reduction of the total power in a circuit. Although the intent is to modify a circuit's setup economically, the processes shouldn't compromise the product's overall quality. With the main goal of enhancing a circuit's efficiency, the other objectives are to increase speed, eliminate possible leakage, enhance power distribution, and improve functionality.

Circuit-level optimization techniques:

- Modification of voltage scales, thresholds, variables, blocks, supplies, and other voltage-related concerns

- Modification and re-sizing of transistors

- Modification of logic styles

- Re-routing of networks

XIII.D. - Interpretation, Analysis & Verification

Although the automation process of EDA tools may eliminate errors in a circuit's system, a product remains a subject of various testing methods. This is due to the industry of circuitry's insistence on guaranteeing the flawless networks of circuit systems. In the aim of making sure that a circuit's functions are in tune with specific requirements, it is interpreted, analyzed, and verified.

In the event when a circuit (that was created with EDA tools) hadn't undergone tests, there is a likelihood that it won't function for a specific purpose. Especially if the project will be employed for commercial agenda, the industry experts are not granting permission to distribute "unevaluated" circuit systems.

Circuit evaluation methods:

- Assessment of a circuit's maintenance requirements

- Inspection of desired and undesired effects (in relation to mathematical logic)

- Inspection of a circuit's functionality

- Inspection of a circuit's stability

- Verification of physical components

- Verification of static timing

Chapter XIV – The Other Way around: Reverse Engineering

One of the coolest ways of understanding circuits is to disassemble all of its components one by one. First, make sure that it is not connected to any power source. After putting on protective gloves, begin taking apart a component; then, determine its function. Repeat the procedures until you know the purpose of the parts and the importance of having them work as a network.

Now, put them all back together; make sure the circuit works.

Such a process is called *reverse engineering*.

XIV.A. - An Introduction to Reverse Engineering

Reverse engineering, also called *deconstruction, reversing, backwards engineering,* and *back engineering* is the process of extracting knowledge from any device or electronic equipment. It involves the need to deconstruct an entire circuit for further analysis of its components. Although the methods that will be employed are opposite to the process of creation, it is considered as a practical approach of learning circuitry.

Moreover, reverse engineering gives light to Aristotle's concept that the key to understanding the operations of a device is studying each one of its parts. Back in the days, the field is limited to its employment on a circuit and other electronic equipment; now, in the modern world, the application of a "reverse" methodology includes almost anything – from children's toys and household appliances to neuroscience, computer programming, and DNA.

XIV.B. - Reasons for Reversing

One of the privileges that reverse engineering can grant to a circuit creator is the guarantee that a device is made accordingly. In the event that he chooses to base his circuit project on another circuit that was created with *questionable privacy*, he can determine any unethical practices. If he takes apart all of its components, he has the chance to have an insider look; by then, he can confirm whether unregulated modifications are in place.

Why use reverse engineering techniques for circuit-creation:

- Documentation purposes – especially in the case of shortcomings and low-quality circuit documentation, the diagnosis of a circuit is necessary to present new information

- Interfacing – with reverse engineering techniques can be subjected to interfacing; it can be evaluated accordingly, regarding its compatibility with another circuit

- Bug fixing – if there are critical faults in a circuit's design, it can be recognized better with a closer look at each of its components; instead of resorting to assumptions, a circuit creator can identify which part of his project needs modification

- Advanced technical information – advanced technical information is rewarded when opening up a circuit; especially for beginners, reverse engineering is a practical way of learning about the straightforward details within the system

- Incorporation of a new functionality – reverse engineering can allow the incorporation of a feature in a circuit; rather than design another circuit, a circuit creator can simply make modifications on his current project

- Modernization – reversing is beneficial in circuitry since it can be used to modernize a project; for instance, if most modern devices are popular in the market due to an innovative feature, a circuit creator can employ reverse engineering to add the same feature to his circuit

- Guarantee product security – if a circuit creator is unsure of the security of his project, reverse engineering is a way for him to determine certain concerns; he can check the specifications of each component and guarantee that none poses safety risks when put to use

XIV.C. – Is Reverse Engineering Similar to Hacking?

Since it is the method for the extraction of information on a circuit that can't be retrieved ordinarily, reverse engineering is argued to be a form of *corrupt hacking*; it is, therefore, a field that a few others in the electronics industry attempt to avoid. However, for many number of circuit engineers (as well as other engineers), there is brilliance in the entire concept of reverse engineering.

According to those who are not against the field, reverse engineering is a way of outsmarting an already finished product; additionally, as they would insist, isn't the point of engineering exactly that – to build and re-build until satisfying outcome is achieved? It may be considered as a form of hacking, but many contest to the idea that it is behind corrupt objectives.

XIV.D. – The Construction of Reverse Engineered Projects

Inarguably, reverse engineering is rather *destructive* and *invasive*. Some are not in favor of it since they do not welcome the idea of tearing their works apart. For others, however, it is a creative way of improving an already completed project; especially if the particular project is outstanding, they are granted the chance to make it even more outstanding.

Among the common projects that can be modified with the use of reverse engineering are *alarm clock radios, coffee machines,* and *colored lamps.* Alongside, the knowledge of internal systems, they can add a unique functionality that is not included during commercial distribution. For instance, you can add a new beeping sound to an alarm clock radio.

For the construction of various reverse engineering projects, it's advised to have a set of tools handy. Prepare a set of *screwdrivers, magnifiers,* and cutting equipment. Additionally, when the disassembly is completed, have a pack of *electrical tape* nearby.

Reverse engineering project tips for beginners:

- Take pictures of a circuit's front and back system prior to disassembly; you can use it as reference

- List down the set of procedures you plan on following; make sure you adhere to them

XIV.E. - Reverse Engineering & CAD

Reverse engineering rode along with the popularity of *CAD or Computer-Aided Design.* Through the years, the field that used to be limited to the basic improvement of a circuit's system began incorporating complex features. It provides a circuit creator the chance to analyze the internal portion of a device.

Moreover, instead of settling on getting a fundamental view of a circuit project that requires reverse engineering, a circuit creator can meticulously analyze a circuit; he can inspect each component thoroughly and come up at the most practical solution. For its development, circuit engineers, circuit designers, and other professionals on electronics started collaborative works with *architects* and those who are skilled in CAD.

Advantages of using CAD technology for a circuit project:

- To improve the alignment of each circuit component

- To enhance the designation of spaces within a circuit's system

- To modify geometric subjects for boosted performance

- To zoom in (and look closely) on each circuit component

XIV.F. - The Legality of the Industry

In light to the different discussions regarding its similarity to *corrupt hacking*, the reverse engineering industry is subjected to various legal complaints. There are even laws (that usually fall under contract laws and fraudulent manufacturing laws) meant for the protection of all sectors that employ *reversed* circuits or electronic devices.

The term *interoperability* is introduced in relation to a variety of legality concerns. With the emergence of cases that revolve around the disassembly of circuit's parts to compromise the quality of a circuit, some who tackle reverse engineered project are not received well.

Reverse engineering is, therefore, only considered illegal if the primary goal is to achieve interoperability. If the goal is for the improvement of a circuit's overall performance, it is encouraged; along with almost every other means of repairing a system, it is even recommended to arrive at a desired purpose.

Chapter XV – Hacking the System

Different communities of hackers host events that give light to those who are passionate in circuitry.

One community, *Artisan Asylum*, hosts a circuit hacking night once a week. In the gathering, circuit engineering fellows – from beginners to professionals, come together to discuss various concepts in circuitry and electronics. There, like-minded individuals share their love for circuitry and talk about their favorite projects, and basically, anything in the world of circuitry.

Moreover, Artisan Asylum's circuit hacking night provides great learning opportunities for circuit hacking enthusiasts. It presents lessons on how to solder, how to use particular computer programs, and how to modify a circuit to function as desired. Apart from teaching individuals the basics and advanced techniques on how to hack a circuit, and have it work as desired, the community encourages the attendees to think outside of the box and come up with brilliant and innovative ideas.

XV.A. – About Circuit Hacking

Circuit hacking, since it is linked with the word *hacking*, can sometimes be perceived as fraudulent. However, there is nothing fraudulent with it since the main reason why there are circuit hackers is for the improvement or the revision of a project; hacking, in this essence, is defined as the modification of an existing circuit to use it for a different purpose. And, in most cases, a circuit hacker is an individual who exhibits cleverness, open-mindedness, and technical aptness.

Due to a few similar concepts, circuit hacking and reverse engineering are said to be one and the same; they are not. While both may include certain techniques that are intended for the improvement of a circuit's operations, the former is merely focused on developing an existing circuit; it may be invasive, too, but it doesn't involve the *deconstruction of an entire circuit*. Especially if it was determined that the installment of a particular component can achieve a desired functionality, having to tear apart the other sections of a circuit is deemed unnecessary.

Common circuit hacking methods:

- Patching – a simple circuit hacking method that describes identifying a circuit's control mechanism or the most integral part of a circuit. Once the main component is identified, you can install a new and better component

- Component replacement – it is defined as replacing at least one component of a circuit with another component that comes with better quality

XV.B. – A Hacker's Main Tool: FIB Technology

FIB or *Focused Ion Beam* Technology is considered as one of a hacker's main tool since it grants him the chance to hack almost any circuit. Ever since the initial introduction of the applications in the 1990s, their usefulness hadn't come unappreciated. The early versions were not only quite expensive, but also, clearly, in need of improvement; later, the tools underwent continuous modifications from many electronics enthusiasts.

According to a study that was led by the engineers at Berlin Technical University, a person skilled in circuitry can install FIB Technology-based applications to hack into a system's security. For the particular research, an IC with low-level security was the focus; the objective was to work around its level of security with the goal of deliberately eliminating its defensive mechanism. The study was, of course, successful and eventually, it was proven that even high-level tools can be hacked with the same practice. And, as it follows, it sheds light on the concept that *there is no such thing as a tamper-proof circuit.*

Moreover, FIB Technology, as a clever technique of manufacturing, developing, and re-wiring a circuit, has earned the approval of different communities of hackers and circuit engineers. Alongside its advantage of boosting a system's performance, it reduces regular operation time. Due to its ingenious way of allowing an individual who's working on an electronic device to design (and even re-design repeatedly) his project, it was subjected to further developments.

Important parts of applications that incorporate FIB Technology (as shown in the layout):

- Aperture – it is in charge of gathering visual aids, then, modifying these tools for a clear display of retrievable information from a particular electronic device

- Deflector plates – it accepts, interprets, then, measures receivable data; initially, it acknowledges all information prior to the screening of the unnecessary ones

- Extractor – it is in charge of drawing out information from an electronic device, then, transferring them to the hacking mechanism

- Lens – it is in charge of making adjustments to assist when processing information

- Octupoles – it is also known as double quadrupoles or octopoles, which means something that has eight poles; it controls beams of ions

- Suppressor – it is designed to prevent power overload due to voltage spikes; it works by regulating the amount of electric current within a system so a device can remain functional

The installment of FIB Technology can be very promising to a hacker

Functions of applications that incorporate FIB Technology:

- Enable and/or disable intruder detection

- Evaluate a circuit's behavior

- Evaluate a circuit's defects

- Gather secret codes and security keys

- Obtain personal details, sensitive data, and proprietary information

- Remove protection systems (e.g. tamper networks, trace meshes, optical sensors, etc.)

- Route incoming data to be received by another network

- Trace and re-trace changes

XV.C. – Circuit Hacking Project

A plus side to the knowledge of how a circuit operates is that you can choose any from your pack of electronic devices and have it upgraded according to preference; the possibilities of its new functions are endless. You won't even have to spend a grand amount, so long as you're familiar with the functions of particular installments. The result of hacking the original system may be rather bizarre, since the product is no longer the same, but nonetheless, the result is likely the way you desired.

In the sample project below, the goal is hack a charger; particularly, modify an existing charger and have it operate with a battery. It can be connected to any electronic device with a USB port. This is useful during emergencies when an electric outlet is nowhere to be found.

Project example (derived from http://www.maximumpc.com): USB Charger with Battery

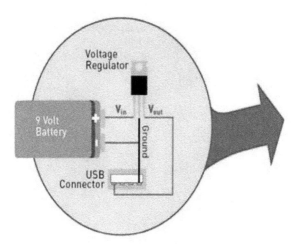

A USB charger with battery can be used for hours (depending on your voltage source)

Materials:

- Charger
- 5-volt voltage regulator
- 9-volt battery
- 9-volt battery clip
- Electrical tape

- USB connector

- Copper wire

Procedures (as shown in the layout above):

1. On a side of the charger, drill a hole for the placement of the USB connector.

2. On the other side of the charger, drill a hole for the placement of the 5-volt voltage regulator.

3. At the bottom center (between the 2 holes), place the 9-volt battery.

4. Above it, establish a ground using the copper wire and 9-volt battery clip.

5. Solder the components together.

6. Wrap the product with electrical tape.

Chapter XVI – Advanced Circuit Engineering: Microcontrollers & Robots

Among the plethora of prospects for a circuit engineer is the opportunity to engage in *circuit-bending* or the art (and science) of modifying existing circuits of electronic devices, and turning them into new musical instruments. In many cases, he isn't required to follow a set of rules for *tweaking* a circuit to incorporate a particular sound; in fact, he can re-design an electronic device as desired.

Alongside, an advantage of circuit-bending is its reward of reducing necessary expenses. In the event that he is very resourceful, the circuit creator can maximize the advantage even more; he can install used (but in working condition) components or less costly parts.

Circuit-bending is merely one of the exciting possibilities for a fellow in circuitry. The options are rather limitless, especially if you let your creativity run loose. So long as you are certain that a circuit will work given a particular arrangement, you shouldn't hold back in taking your beginner's knowledge of circuits to an advanced level.

XVI.A. – A Circuit Engineer's Future in Robotics & Computer Engineering

A reward of being skilled in circuitry is the opportunity to venture into other engineering fields such as *robotics engineering* and *computer engineering*. Your knowledge of how a circuit operates? You can look at it from a brand new perspective; you don't have to be simply in the industry of circuit engineering or electronics engineering. Apart from its offer of a more bountiful career; you can employ it to create a project (or a batch of projects) that you can be proud of. With the mastery of the basic circuitry lessons, delving into related fields becomes easier and more exciting.

With your interest in circuitry, you may seek for other career positions; usually, the employers of robotics engineers and computer engineers welcome circuit engineers into their workforce due to *trainability, familiarity with circuits,* and *good background in electronics.* It may take another set of years of studying, along with new skills to learn, but you can definitely go higher; it takes commitment from your end, too.

Advanced lessons that will be useful for a circuit engineer:

- Integral connections for hardware components

- Software and hardware essentials

- Robotic essentials

- Computer operations

- Computer architecture

- Computer programming (recommended programming languages are C and C++)

XVI.B. – Microcontroller + Microcontroller Programming

A *microcontroller* is a small device that serves as the computer in a circuit; it is a common tool that can be found in *remote controls, smart medical assistance equipment, office machines, state-of-the-art appliances,* and *engine control systems.* With the rapid pace of various information-retrieval operations, its function of addressing *size, cost, time,* and *performance* concerns offers privileges a user with improved overall performance. It is usually implanted on a separate electronic device before or after that device is finished. In certain cases, it uses 4-bit words and low frequency clock-rate operations.

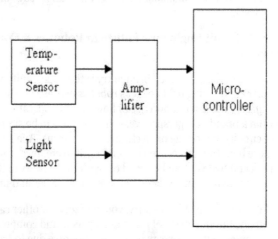

A microcontroller is dependent on a programmer's instructions

Moreover, while a microcontroller is a very useful device, it is only as good as the program that was written for it; this is where the importance of *microcontroller programming* enters the picture. It is a tool that merely executes certain instructions; in the absence of specific commands, it won't function. However, if you design it with even a hundred task capabilities, it can perform each one without fault; granted it was programmed well, it can power a device as desired.

What a microcontroller can do:

- Enable and/or disable clock feature

- Enable and/or disable light capabilities

- Configure audio and video settings

- Add an external monitor

- Automatically detect and/or repair errors

- Automatically update old components

- Magnify an electronic device's performance

- Eliminate unwanted features

- Tighten security features

Example of microcontroller programming:

Result	Microcontroller Programming (in C language)

By tweaking its USB components, a microcontroller's clock setting can be formatted. It is also programmed to activate BL or backlight with a trigger.	for (;;) [
	
	handleserial ();
	
	CDC_USBdevice (&interface)
	
	CDC_USBdevice (&digitalizer)
	
	handleserial ();
	
	]
	
	]
	
	/Setup/ [
	
	int ret
	
	USB_initialize
	
	clock_setup (div1);
	
	BL_off (1), BL_on (0);
	
	ret = digitizer_USB_initialize ();

	if (ret)

XVI.C. – Robots + Robotics

Another way that you can take your knowledge in circuitry up a notch is to consider a career in *robotics engineering*. Due to your familiarity with a circuit, you can begin honing your skills in creating coherent circuits; you can construct a series that is dependent on the individual circuits to deliver its primary function.

As you commit to robotics, like in programming, a lineup of new skills (e.g. artificial intelligence developments, dynamics, motion planning techniques, mapping tactics, etc.) must be acquired, too. This time, other than your hand in circuits and other electronic components, you have to visit aspects in the *mechanical* fields. However, given your exposure to similar concepts in circuitry, learning in the field may not be a challenge.

With your expertise in circuits, you can be behind innovative and extraordinary robotics projects that can be advantageous for both commercial and personal use. It just takes a matter of determination to move forward, and the fact remains that a course in circuit engineering can present you with a satisfying place in robotics, as well as other promising opportunities.

Conclusion

Thank you again for purchasing this book!

I hope this book was able to help you understand the fundamentals in circuit engineering. The lessons shared to you here are meant for a beginner in the subject; the different discussions are written simply. And, so far, it may have dawned on you that there's still more to discover about circuits.

The next step is to learn even more about circuitry and circuit engineering. Especially if you're considering a career in the field, advanced lessons would be good. Since this book has introduced you to the subject, and maybe inspired you to see the fun side in circuits, as well as electronics and electrical engineering, you may want to take the beginner's perspective to a whole other level.

Finally, if you enjoyed this book, please take the time to share your thoughts and post a review on Amazon. It'd be greatly appreciated!

Thank you and good luck!

Book 2
Malware
By Solis Tech

Malware Detection & Threats Made Easy!

Table of Contents

Introduction...91

Chapter 1 - Malware...92

Chapter 2 - Virus..96

Chapter 3 - Worm...98

Chapter 4 - Trojan Horse..101

Chapter 5 - Threats on Mobile Devices......................................106

Conclusion...108

Introduction

I want to thank you and congratulate you for purchasing the book, *"Malware: Malware Detection & Threats Made Easy!"*.

This book contains proven steps and strategies on how to avoid, detect and remove malware.

Malware creators are very creative, employing both technical and social means to spread malware. Simply installing antivirus software is no longer enough. This book explains how malware spreads in order to arm the reader with information on how to manage its threat.

Thanks again for purchasing this book, I hope you enjoy it!

Chapter 1 – Malware

Computers are inherently dumb. They can accept and input data, can process it at high-speed, and can return the results almost instantly. However, users need to tell the computer what to do in the form of codes. We call these codes programs, applications, scripts or software, but they are essentially the same. They give instructions to the computer. What the computer does will depend on the instructions given to it. Tell it to do something useful and it will. Give it instructions to perform a malicious task and it will do it without question. Even computers with artificial intelligence are simply following instructions that simulate human's way of thinking.

Computers do not care who gives the instructions. As long as the instructions are loaded into memory, the computer will process it accordingly. Upon startup, a short set of instructions will tell the computer to load and launch the operating system or OS. The OS in turn executes startup instructions that it finds. These include preparing the input and output drivers, as well as launching other background tasks. Having done that, the OS awaits command from its user to execute other applications.

Malware developers take advantage of these key concepts. They find vulnerabilities in the operating and network system that will allow them to install malware and have it running in the background. Vulnerabilities are bugs in the program that can let malware writers load additional code and execute it. These bugs or programming errors do not always appear during the testing stage.

Some malware writers use social engineering to trick victims into installing malware into their computers. They use the computer's connection to internal and external networks to propagate the malware. They infect shared storage to spread malware among colleagues. They hack into servers to install malicious code that will infect site visitors. They can do this because computers will run any executable code that is loaded into its memory.

What is Malware?

Malware is short for malicious software. It is a general term for a code that compromises a computer and instructs it to do malicious tasks, often without the knowledge or permission from the computer's owner. Early malware refers to programming challenges and pranks like programs that delete user files, but recent malware refers to targeting servers to make them inaccessible or for financial gains.

Home computers are not safe, either. Cybercriminals are using home computers to launch attacks on servers in addition to stealing personal information to access online bank accounts. Some advertisers adopt malware, too. They no longer wait for users to visit their sites, but install malware into a victim's computer so they can modify browser settings and change the default home page, eventually advertising their products every time a user opens the browser. They sometimes change the default search engine, replacing it with engines that track user habits to benefit advertisers.

Mobile devices are not safe, either. Today's mobile devices are computers with features and capabilities that are comparable to older computers. Mobile devices, like smartphones and tablets, are vulnerable because they require applications to work. If users inadvertently download a compromised application, then there is a possibility that malware can compromise their mobile devices, too.

A future malware playground is Internet of Things. It is a term for consumer devices like smart home appliances and vehicles loaded with small computers to provide intelligent functionality. These intelligent appliances connect to the Internet for remote control and administration. Having computers on these things, it may not be long until we can see malware on these devices too.

Remember that appliance manufacturers are not IT companies; hence, they may not have the capability to implement data security in their products. A hacker compromising a manufacturer's server could trigger a firmware update on connected appliances and make it perform additional functions, including attacking other servers on the Internet. It may sound like an event from a science-fiction movie, but this reality is possible.

What is the Difference Between a Malware and a Virus?

Many people confuse malware with viruses. A virus is a type of malware, while malware include viruses and other malicious software.

The first malware were viruses, and developers wrote antivirus software to eliminate these malicious programs. Even when viruses evolved to other forms, people still call them viruses and antivirus companies are using the same term even if they are targeting other malware variants.

Viruses are no longer common on their original form. With antivirus vendors constantly updating their algorithms, malware developers have to come up with new variants to avoid detection, often employing social engineering to propagate malware faster by tricking victims to install it along with legitimate software.

If we look at how malware developers remain active over the years, we can surmise that it is a financially rewarding business; therefore, we can expect cybercriminals to continue developing better malware while antivirus companies play catch-up. The only way to combat malware is to understand the threat it presents, how it spreads and propagates, how to detect it, and how to remove.

What are Potentially Unwanted Programs (PUPs)?

People love free software; however, developers need to earn money too. Malware developers see this as an opportunity to spread malware while providing revenue to free-software developers. What they come up with are installers for legitimate software that also install malware during installation. Antivirus companies call these Potentially Unwanted Programs instead of malware since victims give explicit permission to install them. They have no way of knowing if users allow the installation on purpose or unknowingly installs them.

Why would Users Give Permission to Install PUPs?

Most users do not bother reading user agreements that installers display during installation. Instead, they simply click on the default buttons or press enter. Even if users will read the agreements and prompts, some may not understand the message and assume that they are installing software that is necessary for the main program to work. Unfortunately, PUPs are easy to install, but are often frustrating to remove from the system. Most have more than one instance running such that removing a copy will trigger the second copy to re-install it. Many recent PUPs affect users' browsers, which can be very annoying.

How to Detect the Presence of Malware?

Users familiar with their computer will sometimes notice unusual behavior. Some are obvious, like the browser's looks suddenly changing. Other users may lose their files or the file types are changed. Users may even see system errors that were not present before.

Some changes are not visual, like a program accessing the hard disk and making noise even when the computer is idle. Malware accessing an external server can slow down Internet connection. Infected computers can also be unresponsive when hidden processes are running and using up the computer's memory.

Before assuming that malware may be causing the problem, try restarting the computer and leave it for a few minutes without running any program. If the computer is still slow, then there may be an unwanted background program running, but it still needs confirmation.

On Windows, check the hard disk space by opening any folder and clicking Computer on the left. A hard disk with very little space can slow down the computer and malware may not be the cause.

If there is plenty of hard disk space available, run the Task Manager by holding Ctrl+Alt+Del and selecting it from the menu. Click on the Performance tab and observe the real-time graph. Both the CPU and memory usage should be relatively flat if the computer is idle. An active graph could mean that a hidden program is busy. Click the Applications tab to confirm. There should be no application listed if the user did not execute a program. If there is no program listed and the CPU or memory graph is active then there could be a malware running in the background.

To see the process that is using up the memory, click on the Process tab, then click Memory to display the list in descending order. Check its Image name and description. Right-click on a name, then select Properties to get more details. Use a search engine to validate suspicious names.

The Networking tab can also give clues on the presence of malware. There should be no network activity if the computer is idle. If the network is slow and this graph is active, then a hidden program is accessing an external server or computer.

These are just some ways of detecting the possible presence of malware. Without knowing what the malware exactly is; however, it could be difficult to remove it manually.

Most leading antivirus software can detect and remove malware. For home users, there are free versions available that offer basic protection with the option to purchase upgrades for additional features.

A Note on USB flash drives

With the popularity of USB flash drives, spreading malware via USB is easier. Malware can automatically execute when the user opens a USB flash drive. Once in computer memory, inserting another USB drive will infect it. To prevent this, do not view the contents of a USB flash drive after it mounts. Instead, right-click on the drive's name or icon, then select the scan option from the antivirus. This will remove malware in the flash drive before using it.

If there are signs that a USB drive is infected, but the antivirus does not detect it, install another antivirus program. Some antivirus solutions are not good at detecting USB-based malware.

Antivirus solutions can prevent the installation of malware to some extent. However, there are malware that can still get through if the user is not aware of how they propagate. The best way to prevent malware from infecting computers is to understand how each type works.

The succeeding chapters give an insight into the various forms of malware. It also provides information on how they spread so that users can avoid infecting their computers. Prevention is still the best cure against malware. However, avoiding malware is not easy.

Chapter 2 – Virus

Viruses are the earliest forms of malware and they date back to the time before personal computers became popular. A virus is simply a program that can replicate itself on the same computer. Even without malicious intent, creating many copies of a virus code can quickly fill up the memory and slow the computer down. However, an unmodified virus cannot spread to other computers by itself even if the computers are on a network. Getting the virus inside a computer is the challenge for virus creators.

To avoid detection, virus creators modify legitimate programs by inserting malicious codes. When these programs launch, the virus loads into memory and scans the computer for other executable codes to infect. The virus code stays active in memory until the computer shuts down and the cycle starts again if the user runs the infected program.

Boot Sector Virus

Some viruses attack the boot sector of the computer's bootable disks. The boot sector is an area of a disk that a disk drive initially reads and loads into memory. It contains the startup code that will load other components of the operating system. When the boot sector is infected, the virus loads into memory every time the computer starts, ensuring that it is active without waiting for the user to run an infected program. Since the disk operating system can fit in diskettes in the early days of personal computers, starting a clean computer with an infected bootable diskette can also spread the virus to that computer.

Be Careful when Using Shared Resources

Viruses can spread through sharing. When a user mounts a removable storage media on an infected computer while a virus is active, the virus attempts to infect programs that it finds on the mounted media as well. In the early days, this applies to floppy diskettes and external hard drives, but infections are more common today on flash USB drives.

Once the user connects an infected storage to another computer and runs an infected program, the virus activates and infects the other programs in the new computer as well. This makes users who mount USB drives on shared computers at risk if the computer has no sufficient antivirus protection installed. For this reason, avoid connecting USB drives at Internet cafes and on other public computers.

Even shared documents can carry viruses. Some productivity software allows scripts or macros to automate common tasks. Scripts and macros are small, but powerful programs; hence, they can spread viruses, too. Executing an infected macro will also compromise other documents on the same computer. Worse, sending a copy of an infected document can also infect the receiver's computer.

Are Early Viruses Malicious?

Some early viruses started as programming challenges. There was a game that was named Core Wars where the objective is to create a program that loads in memory, then replicate and terminate other programs running on the same memory space. The competing programs create copies of the code while overwriting enemy codes to terminate them. The program that remains in control is the winner.

Other early versions are simply annoying. Two programmers wrote the Brain virus because users were illegally copying their diskettes. The Brain virus simply displays information about the programmers. The Brain virus spread to computers in other countries.

Computers were not widely connected before and the worst thing that a virus can do is to delete files or make them inaccessible. This is exactly what early destructive viruses did. Some programmers wrote viruses that display something interesting while deleting computer files.

Birth of Antivirus Companies

It was not long before other programmers started writing codes to remove viruses, turning the process into a never-ending game of cat and mouse. Virus creators are continually discovering new computer vulnerabilities that they can take advantage of, while antivirus developers update their codes to combat new virus strains. It has become a never ending battle between malware developers and antivirus companies.

Antivirus programs initially identify specific viruses using their signatures. Signatures are like patterns or fingerprints that identify specific viruses. Virus creators responded by continually creating virus variants that require new methods of detection to keep up. This is why antivirus programs update their databases almost daily.

Antivirus can only play catch up if they rely solely on signatures. Modern antivirus programs detect possible viruses by their behavior in addition to signatures.

Most free antivirus software in the market can eliminate common virus threats so not having one installed is not an excuse. While they retain the name, current antivirus software can detect and remove other forms of malware. To enable additional protection, users can purchase additional features.

However, those who do not have a budget for paid features can still protect themselves from malware. The key is to understand how other forms of malware spread. The next chapters will explain these.

Chapter 3 - Worms

While viruses were a threat due to their ability to replicate, it is not a tool for mass infection because it cannot spread to other computers. The capability to spread over the network by itself is a feature of worms. Networks include local area networks (LAN) that are commonly found in offices, Wide Area Network (WAN) for remote offices, as well as worldwide networks like the Internet.

Early worm research had good intentions and started as helpful ideas. One worm crawls networked computers at night to run processor-intensive tasks, but saves the work and stays idle during the day so people can use the computers normally. It is a good idea that maximizes computer resources, similar to how modern cloud computing works. However, a programming error caused the computers to crash and they had to write another program to remove it.

Another programmer wrote a seemingly harmless worm to check the size of the Internet. The worm creates copies on target computers as it moved from one computer to the next. Due to a programming decision, it can install a copy even if it already exists on the same computer. Multiple running copies of the same worm can slow down the computer until it eventually crashes. A single worm was able to crash a big part the Internet.

Worms spread across the network by exploiting operating system and application vulnerabilities and taking advantage of insufficient data security practices. Nowadays, worms can also spread through social engineering. Social engineering is a technique used by hackers to trick users into unknowingly breaking standard data security precautions. Hackers can bypass a highly secure environment using social engineering.

Operating systems, or OS, are programs that manage computers and network equipment. Just like any program, it can have unintentional bugs and updating usually fixes the problem. Worms take advantage of these vulnerabilities to compromise the system.

If the OS or application developer releases an update before someone announces the vulnerability, then users have time to update the operating system before a malware exploits the vulnerability. This is why users should install updates especially if the patch is to address data security issues. Allowing automatic updates usually takes care of this, although there is a risk of automatically installing buggy updates.

On the other hand, if a malware creator releases a worm before the developer discovers the bug and releases an update, what we have is zero-day vulnerability. Modern antivirus companies address this by developing algorithms that detect malicious behavior. However, very aggressive antivirus solutions may lead to false positives.

False positives result when a scan reports the presence of malicious code when there is none. A good antivirus has few false positives. Third party evaluations can determine effective antivirus solutions with fewer false positives.

Mass-mailer worms

Worms can access email clients on user computers and use it to email copies of the worm to contacts in the address book. Some of these emails can trick recipients into downloading and installing the attachment, compromising the receiver's computer in the process. When this happens, that computer also becomes a mass-mailing tool. Unfortunately, these worms can also get a name from the address book and change the From field with this name. This means that the sender in the email may not be the email source, making the source difficult to track.

Aside from possibly compromising recipients' computers, mass mailers can also slow down network performance. If a worm infects several computers on the same network, then it could eat up all the allocated bandwidth. Worse, data security companies may include the computer's IP address in the blacklist for spamming. This can affect all computers in the network that shares the same public IP.

This is because most offices and home networks use a single public IP address for their router while individual computers get private IP addresses. Worse, some DSL subscribers may get a banned public IP address when their router restarts.

Always be wary of unsolicited emails with attachment even if it comes from a trusted source. A possible indicator of spam mail is when the receiver's name is not mentioned in the salutation. Bad grammar is also a sign of possible spam email.

Do not assume that the antivirus can catch all worm variants. Some worms change the file extension of the attached file. Users may think that they are opening an image file when in reality they are executing a worm. Worms do this by adding a .jpg to the filename, like picture.jpg.exe. Since many users configure their computers to hide the file extension, they do not see that the real extension is .exe because the filename they see is picture.jpg.

Some mass-mailer worms simply send spam advertisements. While they may not do damage to a user's computer, they can still trick victims into purchasing illegitimate products. These emails often have a web beacon, a small image that is loaded from an external server. Displaying this image will send the user's email address to the server, thereby validating that it is an active email account. It will then be a target for future spam emails.

Note that spammers do not use their own computers to send mass emails. They use email worms to prevent authorities from easily tracking them.

Worms for Phishing

Mass-mailer worms provide a great platform for quickly distributing malware. Malware creators use these worms to transport different payloads depending on their intention. One application of mass-mailers is for phishing.

Phishing is a form of identity fraud and is usually for stealing personal information for financial gains. It works this way.

Malware creators will copy a legitimate website's looks, specifically the login and profile pages. Websites of financial institutions like banks and payment platforms are examples of these. Next, they will create an email that looks like an official document coming from the target institutions. These emails often have a sense of urgency, requiring the user to log in to the website immediately to validate or change the password for security purposes. It will also include a link to the appropriate page for the user's convenience.

There lies the trick. Instead of linking to the legitimate page, it will redirect the user to the fake login page after clicking the email link. The URL will have the legitimate website's domain name, but with added characters. Some users may mistakenly believe that they are in the genuine site and proceed to log in. After entering the login detail, the next page may even require them to enter their credit card details for validation.

In reality, users can enter anything in the login page and it will be successful. The login page will simply save the credentials entered by the user, then display a page to get other credentials. When in doubt, users can initially enter incorrect login credentials to check if the site can really validate their account. If it accepts a wrong username or password, then there is no validation and the site is a fake.

Another way to verify if a website is a fake is through browsing all the menus and internal links before entering the login details. Malware creators may not go through the trouble of recreating an entire website's content.

To guard against phishing, never click on an email link to log in or change account details. Always type the known URL on the browser address bar. If clicking an email link asks the user to log in, then do not continue. Instead, type the correct URL in the browser's address bar before logging in.

The next chapter discusses other payloads that worms usually bring.

Chapter 4 - Trojan Horse

Trojans are malware that disguise as useful programs or install together with a legitimate application. Its name comes from the Trojan War, a part of Greek mythology where a wooden gift horse had soldiers inside that attacked the enemies while they were asleep to win the war. Similarly, a Trojan pretends to be a useful application, waiting for the user to launch it to execute the malicious code. Once activated, trojans will run in the background to do their designated task.

Trojans do not replicate and spread by themselves. They often combine with worms to infect other computers. Trojans are also common on unsolicited email attachments, while some users download them along with valid applications.

There are several types of trojans according to function.

Root kits

Root kit is not inherently bad. It is originally a tool for system administrators. It becomes bad if the creator installs it on a computer without permission from the owner, especially if the purpose is to do malicious tasks.

Some trojans will modify the computer's system for hackers to gain access. Root kits are tools for administrators that hide in the operating system while providing a back door for their creator. With privileged access, a root kit's owner can do almost anything to the infected computer remotely. Root kits are good at hiding their existence, making them difficult to detect. They can also delete any traces of malware installation. Root kits usually remain hidden until activated.

Bots

Bots are programs that perform automated tasks. Some bots, called spambots, flood websites with spam advertisements to generate traffic for another website. This is common in online forums and is the main reason why websites validate users before accepting their registration details. Some registration forms require the user to type the characters shown on an image to validate that the applicant is human. However, some spammers go around this by hiring humans to solve the test, although it comes at a cost.

A more malicious bot is one that employs brute-force attack on target websites. Most website owners do not build websites from scratch, but simply use an open source Content Management System (CMS) as a starting point. A CMS is a fully functioning website that allows the user to update content without writing a single line of HTML code. There are many templates to choose from, and websites owners can customize further by using their own graphic images. Using CMS, owners can update website content in a few clicks.

Many CMS software have the default username "admin" and some website owners do not bother changing it. Given the default administrator name, hackers only need to guess the password to take over the website and install malicious software. If it is a popular forum, then there is a risk that hackers can steal the member database.

To attack a website, hackers write bots that log into the target website and try to log in with passwords taken from a table of common passwords as well as words from the dictionary. A website that does not limit failed logins in a given period is a good target. Using a network of zombie computers, hackers are able to brute-force attack a website using bots with minimal risk of authorities tracking the attack's mastermind.

Stolen password databases from forums are not safe, either. Using rainbow tables, hackers can use brute-force to find the matching password for a member account. Since many users employ the same username and password on all sites they register to, this allows the hackers to hack into members' accounts on other sites as well.

Remote-controlled Bots

Malware developers can turn an infected computer into a remote-controlled bot that will perform malicious tasks, including attacking another computer. This is how they get away with Distributed Denial of Service attacks. Attackers do not use their own computers to flood a server, but instead, they use a large network of zombie computers from unsuspecting users. This also saves the attacker from bandwidth costs since the computer owner is paying for it. It also makes it difficult to track the attacker after it spreads from one computer to another.

One analysis of an affected computer shows that bots log into a chat server, waiting for commands from its master. Think of an army of sleeper bots just waiting patiently for a command to attack. Developers will typically just let an installed Trojan do nothing until they have an army of remote-controlled bots to launch a large-scale cyber-attack. The attacker then issues the command to attack from the chat server where the bots log in each time the infected computer is running.

Without good anti-malware software, the presence of a remote-controlled bot in a computer is difficult to detect since it sleeps until a command is given.

Keylogger

Some trojans can capture keystrokes as well as mouse movements in the background without the user knowing it. Called keyloggers, these programs can serve as surveillance software for a good purpose. Some parents use it to monitor children's online activity.

Trojan keyloggers can steal passwords and other personal credentials from unsuspecting users. It can wait for specific events, like users opening a login page, before starting to record user actions and keystrokes. It then sends the log to a remote server for its master.

Spyware

Spyware is another Trojan that collects sensitive information similar to a keylogger. However, it is not limited to monitoring key strokes to steal user credentials, but can also gather information about the user's online activity as well.

Adware

Adware is similar to spyware, but simply records and sends users' online activity and behavior as marketing data to marketers so they can display an appropriate advertisement. Some versions will redirect browser searches to advertisements while others will replace the default search engine with an advertiser's search engine.

Adware creators write these malware for revenue generation. Adware that alters browser settings is very difficult to remove. Antivirus software can remove adware from the computer, but usually leaves the modified browser settings. Saving browser bookmarks and restoring to factory settings can sometimes fix the problem.

Ransomware

Ransomware does what its name suggests. After installing the malicious code, it will either prevent access to the infected computer or encrypt the contents of its hard disk. Users will see a message demanding payment to disable the malware. The criminals behind typically employ money transfer services that are difficult to track. Add this to the fact that these cybercriminals usually live in other countries, making it difficult to run after them.

To spread ransomware, cybercriminals typically take over a legitimate website, usually without the owner's knowledge, to install the malware. They can also spread ransomware using drive-by downloads on the compromised website.

Drive-by Download

A drive-by download will allow the installation of malware by simply browsing an infected website. The user does not even have to click a download link. The affected website contains codes that check for browser or operating system vulnerabilities that allow for automatic download. The malware will install a program with a task to connect to another server to download the rest of the malware. The victim may not notice the download due to the initial programs' small size.

Some anti-malware software can warn if a website has malware when a user tries to access it.

Suspicious Packers

In order to avoid detection, suspicious packers compress and encrypt malware code. Good anti-malware utilities are aware of this and are able to detect the behavior of suspicious packers and prevent them from executing.

Removing Trojans

Most antivirus companies have software that can automatically remove trojans. While it is possible to remove Trojans manually, this may be a challenge since many have multiple copies running that can reinstall copies if the user deletes one.

When looking for good antivirus software, try the demo versions first. If satisfied, users can pay for other features that provide complete protection to the computer. Some of these protections include email and web surfing security.

In some cases, antivirus software can remove malware from the system, but not from the browser. If removing browser add-ons and restoring to factory setting does not work, uninstall the browser and download again.

Avoiding Installer Trojans

Among the popular sources of Trojans are free software installers. Software development costs money, and offering it free is not good for business. However, many people would prefer free over paid versions, especially when performing simple or one-time tasks. To address this, developers break down their programs by specific features, then allow third party marketers to offer them as free downloads in return for revenue to the developer. For example, one utility can convert AVI formats to MP4, while another can convert MP4 to MPG.

How can marketers earn money from offering free downloads? They get revenue by offering their services to advertisers. These marketers create installers for legitimate software, then include the option to install software from other companies. There is nothing wrong with that right, except that many users do not bother reading what they are installing. Unfortunately, many of these optional programs are adware that antivirus software tag as Potential Unwanted Programs (PUP).

An installer for free software will first confirm that users want to install the desired legitimate program. After the user clicks on the Continue or Next button, the installer will get the user's consent to install additional software along with a few descriptions of its benefits. Sometimes, the installer will display an End User License Agreement (EULA), something that no one ever reads, but simply agrees to. It is common to see more than one program added in the installation. The problem, however, is that the default buttons will install these extra programs if the user is not careful.

How can users avoid these additional installations, especially if the user is unsure if the other software is required? Most installers have a Decline button for optional installations. When an installer shows the Decline button, then that additional software is probably a PUP. Pay attention to the presence of Decline buttons.

Some installers have no separate dialog boxes for additional software installation. Instead, easy and custom install options are available, with the easy install as the default. What the user may not see is that the easy install option will sometimes install additional software. Click the custom install option when it is available and deselect unfamiliar applications.

Some antivirus may give an alert that the installer has a Trojan. Always scan the installer after downloading. Users can do this by selecting the installer, right clicking then selecting the Scan option to run the antivirus. This is also a good practice after inserting USB devices.

Users can perform additional verification after each installation. In Windows, simply select Programs and Features from the control panel, then click the Installed On tab. Sort the list in descending order. The programs with the current date are the ones included in the installation. Select suspicious programs and click uninstall. To verify applications, enter the program name in a search engine to see what it does.

Chapter 5 – Threats on Mobile Devices

Mobile technology is now a part of people's everyday lives. Smartphones today are very powerful. They are no longer just for voice and text, but for accessing the Internet and playing games as well. Though not as efficient as personal computers, users can perform most tasks on their smartphones.

For those who require laptop capability at more portable form factor, tablets are a blessing. Those who want the small size of a phone, but with a bigger screen like a tablet, can choose a phablet. Mobile computing is now a reality.

As computers, these mobile devices can be targets of malware. To minimize these, Android and IOS, the leading mobile platforms, have screening policies in place to reduce the chances of malware getting into the official stores. Additionally, updates to the operating system often include security fixes for known vulnerabilities to strengthen the security of devices. Installing the latest updates, when available to the user's mobile device, addresses possible malware problems.

By default, users can only download apps from the official stores. This is Google Play for Android and App Store for IOS. However, a checkbox on Android's setting will allow the user to download from any external server. There lies the problem.

The price for mobile apps is quite low compared to their PC counterparts. However, many users still do not wish to pay for the apps they download, despite their low prices. Malware creators take advantage of this by making commercial apps available for free download on third party servers. By simply deselecting a default Android setting, users can now download a paid app for free.

Unfortunately, for them, these modified apps may contain malware written for mobile devices. Once installed on a mobile device and executed, these malware take over the device and do what PC malware often do. Some malware may steal user credentials while others may display unwanted advertisements. These malware can make the devices very slow, rendering them unusable. Restoring to factory settings may be the only option for some.

IOS has no checkbox to allow downloading of apps from unofficial sites, but bugs in the operating systems can allow jailbreaks. Jailbreaks are IOS hacks that allow users to customize their devices. It also allows users to install unofficial apps. Some of these apps may have malware and can compromise the device.

Malware creators are smart and can always find ways around a secure system. One company created a Windows application that allows users to download apps for free then transfer them to their IOS device. This comes with a risk, however, since some of these apps may also have malware.

106

Malware creators started targeting IOS developers in China. They did this by making local copies of Apple's development platform since downloading from Apple's official servers is quite slow for developers located in China. Unfortunately, the unofficial installer has malware that infects the apps they are developing. Some of these apps made their way into the App Store before they were discovered and removed.

Another malware creator took advantage of enterprise certificates. These certificates are used by companies to install their own apps on IOS devices without approval from Apple. Malware creators are tricking users to install an enterprise certificate so they can install apps with malware on victims' devices. Many users who do not understand the implications are at risk.

Apple quickly released an update to IOS that prevents this malware from installing. Those who are still using an older version of IOS can also avoid this malware by not allowing the installation of certificates unless it is from their company's IT department.

For IOS users, downloading apps only from the App Store can minimize the risk of malware. It does not mean that Android users are safer, though. Malware writers are invading Google Play by creating fake apps that mimic original apps, but with additional malware. Google has to monitor millions of apps and ensuring that apps do not have malware is not easy. There is a way to avoid potential malware, though. If an Android app asks for unnecessary permissions during installation, do not install it.

Fortunately, antivirus companies now have versions for both the IOS and Android platforms. Installing these apps will help users screen potential malware during installation, as well as remove malware that were accidentally installed.

Conclusion

Thank you again for purchasing this book!

I hope this book was able to help you understand malware threats to prevent them from spreading.

The next step is to check your computers for signs of malware and apply the lessons in this book to avoid infections in the future.

Finally, if you enjoyed this book, please take the time to share your thoughts and post a review on Amazon. It'd be greatly appreciated!

Thank you and good luck!